LIVING MYTH
Exploring Archetypal Journeys

Tom Jacobs

Also by Tom Jacobs

*Seeing Through Spiritual Eyes:
A Memoir of Intuitive Awakening*

*The Soul's Journey I: Astrology, Reincarnation, and
Karma with a Medium and Channel*

Saturn Returns: Thinking Astrologically

*Chiron, 2012, and the Aquarian Age:
The Key and How to Use It*

All material in this book © 2007-2010 Tom Jacobs.
All rights reserved.

ISBN 145059252X
EAN-13 9781450592529

Contents

Acknowledgements 4

Preface 5

Introduction 7

Juno and Commitment 15

Pallas Athene and Re-integration 23

Vesta and Her Virgins 29

Ceres: Identity, Loss, and Change 39

Persephone's Ransom 49

Chiron: Difference, Resourcefulness, and Mastery 64

Lucifer: For the Love of God 73

Lilith's Rage and Re-writing History 81

Lilith's Flight 90

Lilith and Seduction 96

Reconciling Adam and Lilith 104

Ariadne and Abandonment 111

Arjunsuri 118

About The Author 149

Acknowledgements

The work in this volume has been made possible by all the people in my life who share openly the stories of their journeys as they live archetypes (usually without awareness of it!), whether family, friends, lovers, clients, or students. All who honor themselves and allow their stories to unfold honor the gods and goddesses in us all, and I'm thankful to them for that. Thanks go to Stephanie Azaria for offering me an online space to publish a number of the book's chapters as a monthly column.

Preface

The Introduction and eight of these chapters appeared beginning in late 2007 on The Cosmic Path website as a monthly column titled "Living Myth." Each of these has been edited and updated, and some have been expanded. Three more (those on Vesta and Ariadne, and the fourth chapter on Lilith), originally planned for the column, are new for this collection. Also new are the chapters on Chiron and Arjunsuri.

Some of the articles include information on the astrology of the asteroids and point in question, and some do not. Even without a knowledge of astrology, this way of looking at myth can help you see the patterns in your own life in new ways.

I've always been interested in the stories of mythology, but my relationship with it began to deepen in my first year of college. It was then that I came across a copy of <u>Bulfinch's Mythology</u> in a used book store in Rowsburg, Ohio, a tiny town near my college (that you might miss if you blink while driving on a country road). A wonderful store that, to me, was full of mystery and possibility. I went there every few months for a few years and never left empty handed.

What I'd previously found excerpted in brief or depicted in books for kids was spelled out, and I was in heaven. I consulted it and bedtime-storied it for years, becoming familiar with many of its stories.

Early on in my practice, I added Chiron and the four main asteroids (Ceres, Pallas Athene, Juno, and Vesta) to my analyses. I heard a lot from colleagues and students about how they understood and worked with them, read books, and developed my own ideas, too. At some point, I began to recognize in myself and others the dilemmas and predicaments of some of these mythological figures.

I began to tell my clients the stories of the mythic figures with whom they seemed closely aligned, and how they could change the stories they were living. I understood that if they were conscious of exactly what they were actually doing (instead of what they *thought* they were doing), they could change the course they were on. It worked fantastically, and has opened many doorways into self-discovery and understanding for me, and my clients and students.

I hope it's as useful for you.

T.D.J.

Tucson, AZ

February 2010

Introduction

Many studying astrology are drawn to include the four main asteroids in their work, yet may not fully understand what to do with them. There are useful books out there on the subject that are worth reading (notably Demetra George and Doug Bloch's <u>Asteroid Goddesses</u>, Red Wheel/Weiser, 2003), but we may not know where to jump into chart analysis after we've read what we can find. This is because we somehow know there's something else going on that keywords and telling of the stories don't address.

What often attracts us to myth is a deep, sometimes unconscious understanding that *we are living these stories*. That, in our lives, we are living out these stories now and, thereby, we are the myths themselves, *we are living, walking myths*.

The stories we're handed down about mythological figures from the Greeks and Romans are often not the whole stories, and do not possibly account for the full measure of attraction we have to incorporating these archetypes into our work (but I mean our lives). When I encountered what's available on these archetypes in the astrological literature, I had a vague feeling of inadequacy of the available information. I don't downplay the work being done or the efforts of those doing it. I mean to emphasize the idea that no book can truly lead a person to understand these areas of his or her life in truly meaningful ways.

In order to fully understand any archetype, we must be willing to see how that archetype informs our lives. We must understand in what ways those stories are our stories. If we don't do this, we run the risk of allowing the rich journeys of individual development that our mythologies offer to become desiccated, ending up lifeless sets of keywords, mere data that are useful only if plugged into a kind of MadLibbish template of astrological analysis: Ceres becomes simply the overprotective mother, Pallas Athene becomes the woman living in a man's world, and Juno becomes merely the vengeful, scorned wife.

There is a challenge for each of us to reconnect consciously with stories we're living. There are different ways to do this, of course, but the first step is to recognize *which* stories we are living. Is there a mythological figure who has always appealed to you? Are you drawn to a particular set of stories from the mythology of one culture or another? The stories we're drawn to are those with which we most strongly identify in some way. Consciously recognizing our attraction to them can open the door to new levels of understanding.

Each mythological figure's story is a journey, a process of unfolding. The desiccated keyword approach fails us because, while through it we encounter some cues we know are part of the story, we find they don't answer what we came looking for: A way of understanding our lives as the unfolding stories we find them to be. It seems natural that we need to have some idea of how to live, to have an example of what to do with ourselves. We search for examples in our mythologies and, to a great extent today, in the contemporary correlate of the oral tales of the past – movies, television and other entertainment media. In other words, we seek a way to understand in what ways we are connected to the collective, and the collective's stories are how we do that.

To find ourselves, we have to find the figures of myth within ourselves. We have to find ourselves in the stories. I've been working with the idea of "living myth" and have been bringing it to my clients for years. My vocabulary and rootedness in the idea deepened and was clarified when I began reading Christine Downing's *The Goddess: Mythological Images of the Feminine* (Continuum, 2000). She offers us an autobiography of her involvement with a few goddesses from the Greek pantheon, those in whose stories she saw herself. She relates how different periods in her life were chapters from the goddesses' stories. Her view is one of myths as alive, and of our unfolding lives as the telling and retelling of myth.

As we live myths, we make them our own. Our experience adds dimensionality to the stories. The collective grasp on the myth is enriched not just when we live one as a portion of our own journey, but when we become conscious of it. You could say that developing a relationship to life is in understanding how we as individuals fit into life. Seeing our lives as chapters of living myths is one way to develop such a relationship, and it's open to any of us willing to take the time to understand our lives as stories.

There's no loss of individuality in such a project, only the chance to of situate ourselves within a larger view. My goal in helping clients to understand their lives by working with them at the level of seeing themselves as living myth is this: *If they can understand the stories they're living, they're better positioned to see how to make changes in their lives, if that's what's needed.* I knew that if they could understand where their choices and experiences are leading them (the ultimate challenge or issue the mythological figure they're paralleling must face), they can be better informed about their options. Not so they know how the story ends, but to gain what knowledge or understanding can bring into focus the arc of the story being lived. Often, it comes out as what knowledge or understanding does the mythological figure need in order to make a choice other than the one we hear he or she makes (that often leads to disaster)?

Myth as Social Instruction

For a society to thrive, it must teach its people to live according to the rules and mores of the group. It has to convey its values in some way, and myth is a primary way cultures all over the globe do this.

Myths as cautionary tales tell us what not to do, or how not to do what we're doing. When people understand how to live the story, yet not come to the same (usually horrendous) conclusion or end – to live the story and choose a different outcome – they grow. They experience a change in consciousness.

Over time, myths change depending on which group is in charge. The set of instructions to be conveyed to the people change with varying political and social agendas. Currently, many people are de-conditioning themselves from what they learned from the patriarchal societies and patriarchal-based religions in which they were raised. One point I wish to make with this book is that there can be a wide gap between a myth that we've received and the archetypal process that humans actually live that corresponds to that story.

All myths of goddesses underwent significant change during the transition to patriarchy. This isn't the place to explore this fully, but several of the chapters discuss how the myth was changed to serve social, cultural and political ends during this transition. In particular, Juno, Pallas Athene and Vesta are discussed in this light.

Myth vs. Archetype

People having experiences that fit along the archetypal arc of a figure's story can be told they're not experiencing what they know they are experiencing, because it doesn't fit with the myth they've been handed down. One among countless examples is that individuals can be empowered and become healthy by living Lilith stories: More connected to their bodies and living with more integrity, developing a deeper connection to nature and themselves as extensions of it. The myth we've received tells us that Lilith is vengeful and bitter, that she rages, seduces men against their will, and kills babies. Obviously, a vast gap between myth and archetype. Will people living the story trust their experience over what they were told would happen if they lived it? Some do and some don't. And yet no matter what you're told, trusting your experience is always a healthier option than trying to overwrite your consciousness with someone else's idea of you.

In some cases, the gap between myth and archetype marks a failure of imagination, but in most it is about planting in our minds seeds of discord with parts of us we might naturally know and trust. With patriarchal forces, it's our feminine sides and, indeed, the Earth itself. The Earth has always been considered feminine, and a successful transition to patriarchy would need to instruct the populace that nature, the Earth, the feminine, and our own bodies can't be trusted. Patriarchy is essentially a campaign to wipe out the feminine in all its forms, yet since this cannot be done, it settles for diminishing and shaming it as much as it can.

The articles in this book address the archetypal journeys associated with real-life human stories, while pointing out the differences between archetype and myth. I do this because in the moment I grasped the difference (and the reason there's a difference), I began to trust myself and my observations of my experience. I wish that others might have the same experience.

You might see yourself or someone close to you in some of the stories you read about here, or you might be stirred to think about the myths you're living and contributing dimensionality to. Perhaps you'll be inspired to develop a vocabulary for understanding your own life as the series of rich, unfolding journeys it is; that at any given time connect you to the greater human community on a level you perhaps hadn't previously seen.

Most of the chapters focus on one part of the archetypal journey. With Lilith, I offer four of main paths along the Lilith journey. The chapters on Ceres and Persephone likewise cover several angles on those journeys. The chapters on Arjunsuri and Lucifer are overviews of those archetypes, and the remaining chapters focus on a single aspect of the journey in question.

Juno and Commitment

Juno as a myth we live involves the unfolding process of learning what commitment is, and the ins and outs of living lives functioning in terms of commitments made. Her story is not merely about marriage, and the asteroid in the chart does not signify merely the spouse or partner. It is about the kind of commitment we understand in terms of traditional marriage, and our experience of choosing and living it. Understanding the realities, complexities and implications of that kind of life whether we marry according to traditional lines or not.

When we hear of Juno as the scorned wife of Jupiter, bitter and wreaking violent havoc in the lives of his illegitimate offspring (of which there were many), we are challenged to dig deeper than that image. Some questions that can come up along this archetypal journey:

- *What is commitment?*
- *What kind of circumstances are right for you to make them? What about necessary? Sufficient?*
- *Are there different kinds, levels of commitment? How do you as an individual understand each?*

- *How do you build relationships with people that reflect and honor your needs?*
- *How do you choose the right kind of people to have the right kind of relationships?*

But let's start with the correlation of Juno with Libra and Scorpio, the signs of two kinds of human relationships. Libra is the sign of one-to-one relationships – any we have with those we perceive as equals. Scorpio is the sign of relationships to which we open up our deeper selves, opening to trust and intimacy – this is where we engage in naked honesty, stripped of all pretense and revealing our intimate selves.

In the natural zodiac, Scorpio follows Libra. In Libra, we're learning to relate to others; about the conceptual framework and then the realities of fairness, equality and harmony. Libra is said to be the sign of balance, fairness and harmony, but the reality is that Libra is the sign of *learning* these things. It is the sign of attempting to navigate the landscape of relatedness. Libra is the first sign in the zodiac that has us taking what we're up to into the realm of other people.*

What ideally transpires in Libra is a bit of push-pull between the needs, wants and realities of self and other between the two people, hopefully teaching each about him- or herself. Relationships happen so people can learn to develop reciprocity, or balance between them. There are, of course, many definitions of equality and fairness (is a relationship wheel greased by a division of labor? If so, how are duties and responsibilities assigned to each person? Etc.). Chances are that when two people get together, notes need to be compared, ground rules agreed to, and perhaps compromises reached. And this is how it's supposed to be: Relationships are major drivers of our change, which is to say our growth.

And then it's on to Scorpio, where we tear off each other's clothes and, um, "know" each other.

Or something like that. Meeting each other in Scorpio has a less-genteel and more business-oriented mandate than Libra, whether or not sex/sexuality is involved, and whether or not the relationship itself has anything to do with sex or sexuality. The essence of Scorpio is in learning just how far we can go into the territory of another before we lose our sense of self. It's not the merging and surrender to the greater whole sought by Pisces, but a desire to get as close as possible to another being. To get inside how the other being feels. (Which is, by the way, all about Source – the energy of Scorpio makes you think you're wanting to get close to another person, but you're actually trying to get close to God/Goddess/Source – the Scorpio part of you is that part that knows that merging with another is actually merging with Source in the form of another person.) Additionally, we've all heard that Scorpio rules shared resources. We all need relationships in which we trust another enough to share resources.

So, given all this, let's turn back to Juno. The relating lessons of these two signs help flesh out the terrain of Juno as an unfolding process, but we have to add more. Essential to the Juno story is that she makes the commitment of her own free will, and expects the man to whom she commits to do the same. When he doesn't, she gets angry.

For Juno, and for those of us creating a Juno story with our lives, part of the healing opportunity is in gaining awareness of the conditions we've attached to the giving of our love. And it *is* after all love that we're talking about here, but an expression of it that becomes to some of us a political gesture, an arrangement. Relationships, after all, are about politics, not love. Love is about love and nothing else, and there are no rules that govern the real thing. Any agreements that we have that seem to be about love are in truth about something else, for love exists outside our particular choices of which humans to give it to and share it with.

There are two nuggets here of what Juno can learn:

1. Love is an active force, and exists outside our selves and choices.

2. Giving is loving if nothing is expected in return.

Love is an active force. Basically, love happens. Love moves us and changes our lives. Love *is*, and love *does*. Love is and does not *because* [insert whatever here] – no, it just *is* and *does*.

Giving is loving if nothing is expected in return. When you expect something in return for your love, you're actually trying to engage in what is tantamount to a business or political partnership. "You scratch my back, I'll scratch yours." Or, more common, "You nurture me like my mom refused to do, and I'll let you avoid talking about and facing your feelings." Or some variant on the exchange principle that holds that there is work to be done associated with the love – that there's a transaction to be had.

Juno gives her complete fidelity to Jupiter and expects his in return, but he never gives it – he is running around getting Biblically busy with just about everything female that moves. Juno will eventually learn that just because one gives something, it doesn't automatically mean that something (of equal or greater value) will be given to her in return – no matter how serious and life-altering the thing being given is, like absolute fidelity.

Going through this process hurts. Let's not forget that behind anger is pain. Juno in the stories lashes out against Jupiter's illegitimate progeny because she's hurting. She feels disrespected, and sees in his behavior what amounts to a deliberate ignoring of her level of commitment to the relationship. That's what she perceives, anyway. What Jupiter's really up to is just doing what he wants: Running around, having fun, getting off. And instead of taking a step back to check in with the obvious reality that they are clearly defining marriage in different ways, Juno lashes out, in admittedly rather creative forms of doling out doom to those unfortunate illegitimate kids of his.

Aside from the opportunity to step back to understand that their definitions of marriage differ, she also has the opportunity to understand the motivations she has for giving what she gives. If her eyes open to what's really going on, she's likely to see that she's giving in order to get. And isn't that more like commerce and politics than love?

I often see Juno's biggest growth opportunity in taking responsibility for having given away her power, and then in taking back her power. The healing shift of those of us living Juno stories seems to me not in seeking revenge when we feel wronged, in thinking our pain and anger are due to the actions of others, or in vowing to stay single and avoid all potential pitfalls of commitment. It's in understanding our expectations of fairness and equality and letting our behavior be guided by our increasing awareness of our motivations, which are informed by our desires and needs.

If you're wondering what taking back your power might look like, I can tell you it likely involves accepting responsibility for how you're creating your life. You need to see with open eyes exactly how it has been so that you can see what is it that you do and learn to proceed with even greater awareness. And you'll need to start with yourself before other people, meaning that you learn to take care of your own needs and *then* go get with someone else you want to share life with.

In a totally unfair, reductionist shorthand that cannot possibly give justice to any of them (see these as a chain, a process or cycle):

1. *Aries = announcement of existence, being*
2. *Taurus = establishment of skills and means to ensure survival*
3. *Gemini = exploration of environment*
4. *Cancer = rooting, nesting*
5. *Leo = learning self-expression*
6. *Virgo = choosing something we can do to perfect*
7. *Libra = taking what we do well to others*

8. *Scorpio = learning what we can and can't do with others*
9. *Sagittarius = seeking truth*
10. *Capricorn = taking the best contender for what's true and manifesting it in the world*
11. *Aquarius = aligning ourselves with others who have the same goals to create the world as we want to see it*
12. *Pisces = surrendering all of our effort, work and goals to a higher something and preparing to Aries again*

Pallas Athene and Re-integration

People are complex.

Wondrously, marvelously complex.

No matter whom you consider, there's a universe inside him or her.

And yet we don't always think that all of us is welcome to come out and play.

Somewhere along the line, for any number of reasons, each of us finds it easier to attempt to shelve a particular part of us that seems to get in the way. This is a normal feature of the human experience, as the complexity that each of us is can't at all times be fully represented in our outward. Just which part of us we attempt to put away again and again is a matter of the journey of the soul, and is determined by a host of factors fitting with what kind of experience the soul has signed up for in the great experiment of this life-on-earth lab course.

Once this part of us is shelved, though, we may in time forget how to relate to it. We might find ourselves misunderstanding how it could even be a part of us. We might even begin to believe that we don't deserve to have access to it, which is in effect saying that we don't deserve to be whole.

But it exists. Others can see it in us, in fact. When confronted by the reflection of it from others, we can be like deer caught in the headlights: stunned, momentarily paralyzed. What trips us up is that we *know* they're right; we *know* that it's true, that it's us. We just don't understand how to be or "do" that part of us. Or, more precisely, how to be or do it and still *feel like us* – still be who we think we are.

One doorway into understanding Pallas Athene inside us is as the part we put away in order to ease a difficult tension that threatens a delicate balance or to succeed at something. It's the part of us that makes the decision to put a part of us on the shelf. It is an attempt to put a part of ourselves on hold.

The part of her myth I'm focusing on in this article is her decision to disavow her connection to her mother, which is simultaneously a divorce from her female lineage and, thereby, her femininity. The story is that her father, Jupiter, swallows Metis, her pregnant mother, and the child is then born inside and emerges from Jupiter fully formed (and, in fact, fully armored).

Interpreting this to mean that the mother was unnecessary and irrelevant is, in essence, political spin having to do with the transition from a matrilineal or matriarchal to a patrilineal or patriarchal social order. The denial is not just of her having been a product of her mother as well as her father, but of the very connection to her female lineage. It's a statement of divorce from the fact of having a female lineage, to being feminine.

There's a price whenever we put a part of ourselves away. In time, whether over the course of one life or many, repeatedly choosing to put a part of our wholeness on hold can result in an apparent divorce from that part. In the beginning it might have been to avoid complication, or for the sake of convenience. For any of us, persisting in a refusal to be our whole selves will at some point become a problem.

The part on hold hungers for attention. After it begins to get attention, it will hunger for public recognition of its existence and importance. We need both to be whole and to relate to other people as wholes, being seen for who we understand we really are.

Understanding what you've shelved and why you've shelved it is the first step to healing the fracture that results from this strategy. Your Pallas Athene by house, sign and aspect will lay out the vocabulary to help you understand what it is. Use the following broad strokes to get an idea of the thematic nature of Pallas Athene through the signs and houses. For each of us, she will take part in a configuration needing more attention to tease out and understand. In other words, here are some notes intended to point in the general direction of where your analysis can go.

Pallas Athene by Sign

Attempted Divorce from a Way of Being

Aries	Instinctual response, unmediated action
Taurus	Grounding, stabilizing, surviving
Gemini	Exploring, opening to new stimuli, curiosity
Cancer	Nurturing, nesting urge
Leo	Playful and authentic expressing, spontaneity
Virgo	Discriminating, analyzing, choosing
Libra	Balancing, harmonizing
Scorpio	Intensifying, intimate sharing
Sagittarius	Intuition and expansion, belief and risk
Capricorn	Planning & building, maturing
Aquarius	Choosing freedom, being original
Pisces	Merging with or surrendering to something greater

Pallas Athene by House

Attempted Divorce from an Arena of Life

1. Relationship with the body, presentation of self
2. Sexuality, survival skills, resources, self-worth
3. The senses and immediate environment
4. Inner life, connection to family/heritage/lineage
5. Creativity, spontaneous expression & play
6. Consistency, responsibility & self-care
7. Fairness & equality, relationships
8. Intimacy & the deep and dark inside

9   Higher thought, religion, guiding principles/law
10 Establishing a public life and reaping rewards for hard work
11 Productive involvement with the right friends and groups
12 Relationship with the greater whole and other realms/versions of reality

Aspects

If she is conjunct a body or point in your chart, this part of your life is what you may find easy to shelve in order to get on with things, or reduce the hairiness of certain situations. Sextiles will tell of a mutual stimulation between Pallas Athene, in any or all of her manifestations, and the planet or point in question. Squares indicate friction between the two players, oppositions a confrontation, argument or standoff, and trines a mutual support and bolstering of whatever they happen to be doing.

Once you can see what yours is, whatever your feelings under the surface about the reality of this part of you, they can offer clues about how to heal this part of you. Time spent recognizing and opening to the feelings that seem the reasons behind your hesitation to allow that part to participate in you openly is the first step in the journey of healing Pallas Athene issues. What's the message you tell yourself repeatedly about why this part of you can't come out and play?

The answer belies a belief that is not based in your present reality, but was formed as some sort of survival strategy in the past, and is therefore a prime candidate for healing in the present.

The opportunity for you in working with whatever your Pallas Athene issues might be is in reclaiming your whole self on a deeper level. Health is wholeness, and to re-meet, re-claim and ultimately re-integrate the part of you symbolized by Pallas Athene in your birth chart is to take another step toward the health of your whole being.

And, in case some Capricornian-Virgoan parts of you are wondering, I don't advocate you let yourself charge yourself with "Attempted Divorce" and enlist your inner judge to pass judgment and impose a sentence – this attempt to shelve and learn about the need for re-integration is all part of the human-life-on-earth show. Treating yourself well and with compassion will go a long way in the healing journey.

Vesta and Her Virgins

The mythos of Vesta as we've received it offers a lot to untangle. In some ways, we don't hear much about her in our traditions. She and what she stands for has been lead to fade out of (Western) collective consciousness in the wake of patriarchal religious traditions seeding themselves and blossoming over the last nearly six thousand years.

As a result, we seem to think we know some about Vesta, but it's wrapped up in confused knots. We tend to have some ideas but lack true understanding of the archetype. Some of what's included here goes back to before Greek and Roman times, as feeling into this archetype requires us to leave behind much of what those cultures added to and subtracted from her energy.

Vesta is the goddess of the hearth, and represents the glue that holds community together. Her temple was the geographical center of a community, and families keeping a fire in the hearth at all times did this in honor of this goddess.

In her temple were priestesses trained in arts that helped keep the community healthy and united. Part of this work was in initiating young men into sexual maturity, and another part was healing soldiers as they came back from war, before they were permitted to re-enter the community.

That sexuality is a major part of Vesta's social functions is why she's been edited out, diminished and twisted around by the patriarchal religions/societies that have thrived over the last few thousand years. A major goal of the patriarchy is to direct and control procreation, with the bottom-line goal of directing and controlling the inheritance of property. Any goddess who is directly involved with natural expression of human sexuality would then have to be displaced, turned on her head or twisted, or edited out of the mythological pantheon by patriarchal forces. We can't have people accepting and respecting their bodies and their natures, now can we? Patriarchy can't take it. It wouldn't survive more than a few years.

The stories of all the goddesses that we've received have been altered on their way to us as, again, myth is a tool for social instruction and we've been instructed to be good little members of the patriarchy.

What's a Virgin, Anyway?

The old-time definition of this word is someone who does not belong to anyone, is not beholden to anyone. How we understand it today is a result of patriarchal influence. Our consciousness of all things sexual has had to be shaped into manageable form in order to get us to deny that our natural selves are okay as they are, as the patriarchy requires this to survive.

The virgins in the temple of Vesta fulfilled an important role in the life of the community, serving sexually in critical ways but also holding space for the reality of this part of our natures. When you read the words *serving sexually*, I'd be surprised if part of you didn't have a little stumble over the concept. If so, you've been trained well to be part of the patriarchal machine. Some part of you has adopted its imperative to attach shame to sexuality and make lots of ways of thinking about and doing sex taboo. The idea that sex has or could have anything to do with healing is supposed to send a panic up the spine of good little Westerners.

Sexual Initiation

The health of a community is determined by the health of its members. As ancient (pre-Greek and Roman) peoples weren't afraid of human nature, sexuality was not ignored or overlooked, with much fear and taboos attached to it. In order for a community to have healthy adults, people had to be initiated into maturity in appropriate ways. Cultures in which sexuality is honored will therefore include initiations into sexual adulthood.

This task was part of the priestess' duties. This is where the idea of a sacred prostitute comes from, but I mention it only as reference. The term is a patriarchal means of diminishing the valuable services these priestesses offered the community, as well as the empowering and healing nature of sex itself. Conscious and intentional use of sexuality was/is a means of connecting with the goddess, and important in the health of a community as a whole.

When it was time for a young man to come into his own as an adult, part of the experience would be initiation at the temple by a priestess. And it wasn't just that he went there to have his first sexual experience. The priestess would be older than him, and he would receive an energetic transmission from her that set him on his way to integrating his budding sexual energy into his self as a whole. The transmission would support him in aligning his sexual expression with the energies of the goddess. This would enable him to participate as a man in his community in healthy, supportive, and productive ways.

The energetic experience of sex is powerful. Imagine that sort, level, and intensity of energy with a pre-set intention of doing something valuable for the health and strength of the community!

Sexual Healing

The community understood the effects of war on those it sent off to fight on its behalf. The community took responsibility for having sent them to war, and being cleansed at the temple before re-entering society (including seeing family) was a requirement for those returning.

Using sex for healing might make an obvious sense, but what might not be obvious is that a priestess was trained to take in and release or transmute the energy from those returning from war. All the fear and anger and trauma in a person's system could be removed by a skilled healer. A few years ago I did a reading for a woman who, I learned when looking into her past lives, had lives as such a priestess. She had karma of not fully integrating or releasing what she took on from men in that role. At the time of her session, she'd been having serious health issues with her reproductive organs, including some scares and surgeries.

I saw that in another life, she didn't trust herself about when she needed to stop doing that work to care for herself. Periodic rests are necessary even for such healers who are expert at managing the energy and taking care of themselves. The Vesta in her got out of balance because she saw the healing needs around her as more important than her own needs. She was still carrying the energetic and emotional garbage of other people, feeling that the service of doing so was something very important to her path. She had identified as a healer in those other lives, and in this life she didn't know what she should be doing to help herself heal. Her route to healing in this life lay in committing to not taking on others' energy (in any way) before she heals herself.

Sexual healing happens and is very important, and there are practitioners out there today doing sacred sexual work. They understand and are trained to manage energy and care for themselves in deep ways.

Sexuality and Shame

The shame surrounding sexuality so prevalent in our world today is in part a result of the patriarchal control mechanisms designed to ensure the appropriate inheritance of property. To get us to accept their ideas, the culture shapers have had to tell us that just about everything about our natural sexuality is wrong unless we're in partnerships sanctioned and controlled by them, and getting busy in ways and with people that they approve of. It's pretty obvious to many that these messages have been delivered via religion, and even some who weren't raised to regularly attend ceremonies in houses of the gods of the patriarchy might have absorbed some of the attitudes of distortion and repression that goes with it.

All distortion engenders pain, and unhealed pain can lead to rage. To heal rage and pain surrounding sexuality, I've found Vesta and Lilith important. Doing each healthily requires us to make peace with our true natures and choose to make choices based in love for ourselves, instead of hatred for ourselves that's rooted in who we've been told we are.

How We Live Vesta Stories

Very often I see Vesta as lending a seriousness, a what I call *religiosity* to what it touches in a person's astrological birth chart. If we allow this part of ourselves to develop, we bring into consciousness a part of us with the capacity to be totally devoted to a cause or way of being. There is often a moral sense to it too, yet when authentic, the sense of morality comes only from inside a person.

Some of us understand the healing power possible through conscious sexuality, and some of us are drawn to sex as a healing modality for ourselves and for others. And for some of us living Vesta stories, we might choose a profession that addresses the healing possibilities inherent in sexuality. In these times of coming out of the grip of patriarchal distortion of sexuality, those who do so go against the grain. There are also people who know in their bones that sex is healing, and yet haven't been taught in this life to approach it with consciousness and intention, leaving them confused about the unhealthy (energetic/emotional) effects sex can leave them with. And as illness follows energetic imbalance, spiritual issues that manifest in a person as sexually-transmitted diseases can be healed by addressing and healing the Vesta archetype within that person. Vesta can teach us to honor ourselves first on all levels, and holds space for our use and experience of sexuality to be infused with the energy of holiness, as we understand ourselves as sexual beings from a more conscious, spiritual level.

Some people work in the healing professions generally, and others are engaged in some sort of service-oriented profession. It can happen when we live Vesta stories that we don't spend a lot of time thinking about *what* we're serving, we just know we need to serve something.

In the daily lives of people living Vesta stories, there's often a willingness to do more for the thing or people we serve than is healthy. The religiosity that Vesta can inspire in us might lead us to be less than picky about what it is that we serve. We need something to be important. We need to feel useful in the service of something we find important.

The learning/healing process with this archetype involves becoming virginal ourselves, using the old-time definition. If there's any excess in our commitment to serve along Vesta lines, we have to learn to be that committed to ourselves first. Whatever service we might want to offer the world or others, we have to learn that serving ourselves first is the key to being able to do it well and healthily. In other words, we have to choose to be beholden to no one, to belong to no one but ourselves.

If your health on any level isn't in order, you won't be clear enough to offer what's truly useful to others and that inspires Vesta's religiosity in you. The archetypal process with Vesta therefore includes orienting to a deep honesty with one's self about one's priorities, and being willing to redefine what it means to serve. Many unconsciously believe that in order to serve well, we have to sacrifice something of ourselves. That we have to give something important up. Vesta teaches us that there are many ways to serve in support of a community, and that there are many ways to think about what service is.

Unwind what you've learned from your patriarchal upbringing about service and sexuality, and you'll be on your way to creating space within you to make your own decisions about these things. Doing so with honesty about what you feel is worth serving will take you into the space that Vesta holds for us to work toward cohesiveness in our communities and the world.

Dedication and the Power of Choice
Underlying all Vesta stories is choice. What a person serves and how one does it comes down to choice. Vesta's priestesses were chosen as girls to spend a

thirty year term of service. If successful in their training, they lived lives of devotion to the goddess, which is to say a life focused on her and the health and stability of the communities in which they lived. You might think that they didn't have a choice about serving, but once they were chosen (by the goddess – an honor for any girl in those times), they made a commitment to that service.

We generally don't grasp how powerful we are when we put our attention in one direction over all others. Many of us have been trained to use our brains to guide us. Others are taught to lead with our hearts, and still others to lead with some lower chakra energy. The power of intention belongs to the sixth chakra, also known as the third eye. It is this energy center that is related to gaining clarity of mind and intention, and putting mind and intention in a particular direction.

The single-minded nature of Vesta and those who live her stories in healthy ways is the projection that emanates from the sixth chakra. If we can accept the power of our minds and intentions, we can learn to live lives rooted in conscious, clear intentions. Living with clarity of purpose and direction brings a person to be the kind of Vestal virgin who serves to bring the holy into daily life, and serves to bring cohesion to the world around him or her.

Ceres: Identity, Loss, and Change

"Identity, Loss and Change" sounds like more than one aspect of a myth, I admit. But bear with me. A major thing Ceres is headed to learn (or needing to learn) in us, *as* us, ties these three things together in one gesture.

Identity, or "Look at All I've Done for You!"
The part of Ceres' story that offers the spark for this chapter involves her role as mother to Persephone (I seem to use the Roman *Ceres* and Greek *Persephone* – perhaps you can forgive me my Mercury-Neptune wandering/name substitutions). The story we know the most about Ceres is of her in that role. Persephone is wandering about with her wood nymph gal pals, picking flowers and frolicking in the fields, and spies a particularly beautiful flower. She stops to admire it, unaware that it was dreamed up and planted in that spot just so she'd tarry…so she can be abducted by the Lord of the Underworld (!), Pluto. You know the one – he lives in hell, but that should probably be capitalized, such a dark and serious place it is – *the realm of the dead*. She hangs out there as his captive for a while, with him saying she's his bride and intending that she stay forever and ever and ever.

Skipping ahead past Ceres' monumental objection to this kidnapping and a rather noisy summit with some other gods wherein she tries to get the marriage undone: Persephone has to spend a third of the year underground, as Pluto's queen. When she was there, you see, she ate a pomegranate seed offered her by Pluto, in effect making a deal to be his bride. The deal is done and she has to live up to it. The other part of the year, to her mother's relief, she can head back above ground and resume life as normal (as if that were possible).

If you've noted that just about everything written so far is about Persephone, you're on your way to getting the thing that Ceres needs to learn: She defines herself in terms of what she does and has done for her daughter, and she defines Persephone as someone for whom things need doing, but really for whom she needs to do things.

For any of us living this story, defining ourselves in terms of what we do for others and defining them by what we do, there's a knot to unravel to be filed under "right nurturing". All parents navigating parenthood explore this issue, of course. What's necessary, what's enough? There are a zillion questions parents consider that boil down to this. But this is about how we, as we live Ceres' story of exploring appropriate nurturing-relationship boundaries, can get ourselves out of where she gives herself so much grief. So, I have to ask, where is it that we-as-Ceres lose perspective? What can a person-as-Ceres gain awareness of to change how the story turns out? But first, there's something important about how *she* lives it.

One thing about Ceres I think about frequently is that she can find herself in a state of wonder at the miracle of creation, of creativity. But also there is wonder in which she can find herself when deeply taking in the reality of being an agent of birth, and standing up within that identity. She may think she's the appointed agent of creation in the birth of Persephone (regardless of the circumstances leading up to or of that birth), and there is a sense of feeling that the self is an all-important agent for the continuation of a life, but perhaps also of *all of life*.

Who among us who's felt this would not take it seriously? Who could avoid flirting with taking pride in that role? Who would not be simultaneously humbled and honored beyond compare to be such an agent of life? Emboldened from such a magnificent sense of purpose?

Now, Ceres is the harvest goddess, the goddess of the grain. We might think that if anyone should or could feel a right to aggrandize herself for her creative prowess, it would be her. But what she rules over on Earth, an ongoing process of change, is something she's not fully prepared or willing to experience in her own life.

I don't downplay the importance of Ceres' experience, or any of her feeling about being an agent of creation/creativity. But there's something she needs to learn, and if you're living a Ceres story in your life, let what I offer here seep into you, find a place in your emotional innards and let it rest there.

Loss & Change

Ceres believes she loses her daughter, but she actually loses her ability to maintain (cling to?) an outdated idea of herself. She loses the ability to keep herself from recognizing and accepting that things change.

Ceres as we live her must learn to find purpose not in the hope that her relationship with her daughter remains static, or regresses to a time when it defined her in a way more attractive to her. She has two jobs:

a) To learn to put into context her role as mother and honor its importance – that all of life continues in this way and that functioning as a part of the grand cycles of existence matters, yet

b) accept that everything changes, and everything dies. And that along the way, each person is supposed to have his or her own direction, sense of purpose, and way of finding a personal connection to life – each of us has the desire, and many would argue right, to self-define, to

When a client comes to me with a Ceres-inspired issue needing resolution, chances are he or she is focusing his or her nurturing energy on other people. It's natural enough to want to help and take care of others, right? There's usually a question echoing inside them: If you understand what other people need and are able to provide it, what kind of person are you if you don't provide it? Very often, though, people living Ceres stories need to learn that you can't save anyone else from making the mistakes they may make – there's only one person any of us can save.

Be a parent or mentor or teacher or helper for as long that's needed, and then let it go. After we've done our part, the best thing we can do for someone we care about is to send them on their way with gratitude for co-creating a space in which we can express our nurturing sides. That's right. We need to thank them for helping us see and get to know an important and wonderful side of ourselves. We're all exchanging these favors, in case you hadn't heard, simultaneously being teachers for each other in all our relationships.

Self-care First

Self-care before care for others might seem absurd or silly to people living Ceres stories, but it's precisely what needs to be learned. In the natal chart, Ceres' placement indicates where our nurturing energy most freely flows, how we most desire to express nurturing energy. It shows us what we think nurturing is. Our Ceres configuration will also indicate in what ways we might tend to care for others instead of ourselves. These are two sides of the same coin, after all – the internal reality manifest in our external lives.

Often, someone unhappily living a Ceres story can see how to turn things around by understanding how it is he or she overlooks self-care. Redirecting the focus to one's self, in other words, changes everything. Oh, the world can seem to threaten a dramatic and terrible crumbling if we have made our purpose about being for others and suddenly have to look at ourselves. But it doesn't crumble. We just have to learn new ways of participating in the world. I can guarantee you that being yourself first, and then being with and helping and caring for others, is a lot more fun than living as though you exist to make sure others get their lives in order.

And when you ask Persephone if she wants to live in her mother's shadow, she tends to answer in the affirmative only if her mother-as-vengeance-fueled-goddess might overhear. But does anyone really want to live in someone else's shadow?

The Astrology of It
Your Ceres sign is how you're inclined go about expressing this nurturing energy, and your Ceres

house is the arena of life in which it is most visible, where it be most apparent. Natal aspects to Ceres show the other parts of you involved in conversation with Ceres, and the kind of aspect tells us about the energy behind their interaction. If you're looking to get a handle on your Ceres placement, you can at look up keywords for the signs, houses and aspects and start making sentences from those nouns, verbs and adjectives.

One woman I've worked with has Ceres in Scorpio at the end of the 6th house, conjunct the Descendant. She's in the process of learning when not to assume that someone needs help. Scorpio's sensitivity to emotional information in others does give her input as to what's happening with others, yet when she does something for someone without that person asking for it, boundary issues (Ceres on the Descendant) can get triggered. She doesn't always understand that just because she can see a problem in another, it doesn't automatically need to be fixed by her, no matter how much she understands about it and how much hands-on knowledge she might have about it (6th house).

Another woman has Ceres conjunct Venus in Libra. As Libra is oriented toward the needs and realities of others, she's aware that she's learning to care for herself. Around the time she had a session with me, she began taking steps to address some health issues that had previously seemed less important than what was going on around her, and what others in her life needed. She'd begun to see that all the things she was doing for others were exactly what she needs to do for herself.

Summary

There is a side of Ceres in anyone living this myth that believes that people we birth, nurture, or in some significant way assist are identified by what we have done for them. Conversely, there is a side of Ceres in any of us living her myth that defines ourselves in terms of what we do for other people.

Either way, there is some confusion of *doing* with *love*. Love does often lead to doing, but if we allow our definitions of love to rest on what others do for us or on what we do for them, we're going to miss the mark and create all manner of unhappiness for ourselves.

I find particular significance in this story. This one has at its central theme something all of us can relate to on one side or the other – everyone comes from somewhere. Each of us is birthed into the world by a woman (at least as of this writing - 4/22/08, 6:24 PM PDT), and that woman has a relationship with the notion of having birthed us, not to mention her feelings about having done it. I believe that even if we haven't actively lived a Pallas Athene story or a Vesta story, or any others, we've lived a Ceres-Persephone story. Because we come from somewhere (someone); we have no choice.

Consider what relationships in your life might offer Ceres-inspired speed bumps, and see what it's like to open to allow them to change, to get into the present, honoring each party's need and desire. Allow your relationships to evolve to serve you in better, more appropriate ways.

Persephone's Ransom

A chapter on Ceres begs to be followed by one on Persephone.

Persephone is the daughter of Ceres and is essentially the perfect daughter. She does what mom tells her and in return is supported in living a perpetually puerile existence. Until something happens, that is. Something terrible and dramatic that causes her to have to grow up and start being her own person.

Here's the story: Hades (a.k.a. Pluto), the Lord of the Underworld and King of the Dead, notices Persephone and takes a marriage-minded, Lord-of-the-Underworld sort of interest in her. Being the honorable type, he approaches her father (who's also his brother) Zeus to ask for her hand. Zeus knows mom (Ceres) will never go for it, so he arranges that Gaia invent and place in Persephone's way the most beautiful flower, knowing that Persephone as a virginal maiden is all about, and will be totally captivated by, a most beautiful flower – especially one she's never seen before.

One day, Persephone is wandering about with her wood nymph gal pals, picking flowers and frolicking in the fields – a favorite activity. Everything's like it always is, with the puerile innocence that fills their days reigning supreme. But then she spies a particularly beautiful flower, a kind she's never seen before. She stops to admire it, unaware that it was dreamed up and planted in that spot just so she'd tarry…so she can be snatched away by Hades. What happens next is pretty typical: a crack in the earth opens up and Hades emerges, driving his chariot drawn by four black horses (I want them to be breathing fire, but I can't find a source that says they do) and snatches her, taking her below the surface to be his bride.

She spends some time down there as his captive, and then Mercury is sent to retrieve her. Just before she goes back to the surface with him, though, Hades offers her a pomegranate seed (or six, depending on the source) and she eats it. Unbeknownst to Persephone, eating something down there means you have to stay – it means you choose to belong down there. Eating food offered by the Lord of the Underworld turns out to be a contractual-type gesture.

Ceres freaks out that her daughter's been taken. The being she believes she exists for has been nabbed. There's a huge and noisy powwow with some other gods wherein she tries to get the marriage undone. But it can't be undone – she ate the seed of her own volition, in effect making the deal. The result is that Persephone has to spend a third of the year in the underworld, as Hades' bride/Queen of the Dead. The other part of the year, to her mother's relief, she can head back above ground and resume life as normal (as if that were possible…).

Some Threads in Persephone's Story As We Live It
Not everyone will experience all of these situations, but if we're living Persephone's story, chances are that we'll live at least one.

Living in the Mother's Shadow
Everyone's done this at some point in life. It's a part of what we do. We choose to emerge into our own world at various times for our own reasons, and with varied results and varied reactions from mom (or the mother figure).

In the last chapter we looked at the need of Ceres in many of us to learn to accept that all relationships change, and to appreciate them as they are while they are. Persephone can learn that while mom's shadow can be a convenient place to remain safe, we might use it to keep ourselves from seeking our own ways of living. At some point the pressure to find our own way in the world will take us far enough away that mom's shadow can no longer cover us, even if we wish it.

Betrayal by the Father

This happens when dad (or a dad figure) arranges for something to happen to us that is not what we would plan for ourselves, and we are in some way hurt. Such betrayals don't have to be as terrible and dramatic and traumatic as possible, but they of course can be. This can also be experienced as a greater scheme by trusted others to usher you into a new way of being, perhaps against your will.

Abduction

The realities of adult life await all even close to what we consider the age of adulthood. Eventually, one of a couple of competing, simple truths that can argue within us prior to our abduction gives way to the other. First, via our parents or those serving as parents, we may live in a state of protection from the harshness of the world. Second, we need to learn how to navigate the world of adult reality at some point. We usually do not learn about most aspects of adult life from the people who are terrified we might grow up and ruin our lives by making mistakes. But we have to make our own decisions and learn our own lessons, don't we?

Note One: What Are You Available For?

There's a thread in all this about what we make ourselves available for. Our abductions have much to do with the unfolding journey of our lives as souls-in-human bodies. Said another way, they have much to do with our karma. I work with karma as accumulated beliefs that are so ingrained in us, rooted so deep inside us, that we attract experiences to make them manifest in the day-to-day world until we change our beliefs. There's no grey-bearded, marble-enthroned figure handing out gold stars and demerits for our behavior, and so even if we experience our abductions as negative and painful, they are in no way punishments.

Note Two: On Violent Abductions

Many abductions into adult realms of life and sexuality are far from positive. The prevailing cultures we live in have all but forgotten how to relate to sexuality in healthy ways, and as a result we do not initiate our young people into a healthy understanding of sexuality. Confusion results as we attempt to find our way into mature embodiment and expression of ourselves as sexual beings, and this is often acted out as sexual violence, and a number of Persephone-like abductions do involve rape.

While not relieving individuals of responsibility for their behavior, we must open to see the prevalence of sexual violence as a symptom of a cultural sickness. It's rooted in frustration from not being initiated into healthy modes of sexuality, from having healthy models of self-acceptance and self-love. As long as we continue to deny the importance our sexuality has in our overall natures (and therefore health of our whole beings), many Persephone-related abductions can involve sexual violence.

Whatever the nature of the realm into which we're going to be abducted, we can spend years waiting for it to happen. Persephone was essentially an adult at the time of hers, and as we live it, the new way of being we're waiting for someone else to come along and sweep us into isn't necessarily premature.

What Happens if You're Not Abducted

Tension builds because you know you're missing something. You know something's off, you don't feel right. You're going about your business feeling less than whole, and you're consciously or unconsciously on the lookout for a person, group, cause or ideal that seems an embodiment of what life should be like. From the outside, it might look like a dreaminess/fantasy world existence, a youthful indulgence. But on the inside, it's a craving to grow up and be initiated into the greatest sense of wholeness we can imagine, in fact can sense in our bones long before we have it or come close.

Any of us can remain in this state for a long time, until maintaining our foothold in our particular version of innocence can simply no longer be done.

What Happens if You're Abducted
Life changes. You're ushered into a new way of being, and whether your personality likes it or not, your soul is experiencing exactly what it needs to.

What We're Learning When We Play Persephone
We-as-Persephone are learning about maturity, both in what is perceived to be mature and how one goes about being mature. Other people's opinions, hopes and dreams about the development of the courses of our lives should cease to matter when we begin identifying as adult agents in charge of ourselves. Living a Persephone story means at times finding out that what others opine, hope and dream about for us that just won't cut it, and we have to figure out how to strike out on our own and learn self-determination.

What you want for yourself is very likely at least moderately more exciting and interesting to you than what a protector figure could dream up for you. But the real point is that your idea of yourself and your life, and what you'd like to do with each, *is yours*. We can persist in doing what the protector figures would for whatever reasons prefer we do, and yet we're not then living our own lives.

To Persephone's Aid

So, then, with the Persephone chapters in our lives, we're talking about becoming self-determining adults, or self-reliant in a new way or to a greater degree. It's harder for some than others, and when we see the harder kind of story being lived by someone, it's important to let go of judgments we might have about where they should be and what they should be doing. Part of assisting anyone to reach new levels of maturity is in becoming grounded in a healthy understanding that sometimes the best help we can give others is to limit the assistance we offer either in type, range or availability.

Since Persephone stories are about self-determination and embracing new attitudes of self-responsibility and self-reliance, we can sometimes wonder how to help someone get through a sticky Persephone story. We can watch people linger a few inches before taking much-needed steps into self-reliance and maturity, with that foot into the future hovering...hovering...hovering...and it can drive us nuts to watch them do what we think is waste time and energy by not moving into the kind of future they clearly would rather be living.

As friends of Persephone, we have to leave her to her quandary and hesitation. The best thing we can do is to listen to her recount her internal argument, and yet it's true that there comes a time when we'll need to stop doing that, too. In cases where you can see a grand windup to a posthumous dead horse-beating in/for/by/of a friend, you can let him or her know you're not available to hear it if you're not. But the most important thing by far, whether you listen or not, is that you approach him or her with love, that you hold a space of love for this process of becoming he or she is engaged in. Because what we're really talking about is self-responsibility and maturity, what Persephone can be hesitant to step into fully, is self-love: Taking responsibility for loving and caring for herself. Having an example of self-loving friends and family members goes further than anything to support a Persephone in your life who's hemming and hawing about taking his or her leap into a new way of being.

If the Persephone in your life is in your family, and is your child or child-figure, understand that the example that you can offer of self-responsibility and maturity is the best you can do. Remember that Persephone's mother's model of love and responsibility is to worry about what everyone else is doing, and that our Ceres placement indicates where in our lives we could use the prioritization of self-care over care for others. When any of us lives a Persephone story, the best help we can get is in finding a model of mature relation to self that has appropriate boundaries, priorities and, care.

Persephone Astrologically

Houses

Where your Persephone (asteroid 399) falls is where this dialogue plays itself out. In what arena of life will (should) your abduction occur? What are you hoping to be initiated into so you can feel more real, alive and fulfilled? Where could you use a self-love kick in the pants into maturity? Check yours out by house, sign and aspect. The house will indicate the arena of life one part of you may tend to remain perpetually puerile, the part of life you may perceive you need someone else to abduct you into a rich, full and more relevant experience.

1. Physicality, taking yourself out into public, asserting & presenting yourself
2. Value-based living, sensuality, self-esteem
3. Curiosity, openness, freely sharing via communication
4. Being in touch with your roots, your true feelings, building a personal foundation
5. Creative self-expression, playfulness, spontaneity, fun
6. Responsibility, duty, service, analytical awareness and related action
7. Learning to create harmony, fairness and balance in relationship
8. Deep honesty, trust, intimacy, intense bonding/sexuality with another

9	Developing a guiding principle for life, use of intuition, risking making life better
10	Ambition, achievement, reputation, social status
11	Goals for the future, working with like-minded others
12	Surrender to something greater, connectedness to all of life

Signs

Your Persephone sign shows the method and motivation of this part of you. It's the mode of being into which you might be waiting to be abducted and, if no one shows up, you'll eventually see that you have to take responsibility for on your own.

Aries	Directness, assertiveness, protective, boldness, bravery
Taurus	Conscientiousness, stability, self-confidence
Gemini	Openness, flexibility, curiosity
Cancer	Rootedness, emotive, connectedness
Leo	Creatively expressive, performing, proud of yourself for what you can do
Virgo	Analytical, committed, responsible,
Libra	Fair, balanced, exploring give-and-take, a good listener
Scorpio	Intense, powerful, absolutely honest, transforming/transformative

Sagittarius	Hopeful, risk-taking, expansive, believing
Capricorn	Constructive, sacrificing, mature, physically productive
Aquarius	Forward-looking, different, original, objective
Pisces	Going with the flow, opening, absorbing, surrendering

Piece together your Persephone house and sign to get some words for what you're hoping to be abducted into, have been abducted into or need to abduct yourself into. While the house and sign keywords above are limited, inserting each of the house and sign keywords will give you something to go on. In other words, while we are marvelously complex as individuals, when the themes of our lives are boiled down to house and sign keywords, there's always a lot to begin working with. Again, this is to stimulate you to begin your dialogue with yourself.

Here's a handful of examples:

Libra in the 2nd: Achieving balance in your self-esteem.

Gemini in the 1st: New and different ways to use your body and show yourself.

Scorpio in the 4th: An absolute honesty about where you come from and your deepest identity and needs.

Virgo in the 7th: Taking responsibility for your relationships, both in choice of relationship and how they work.

Aries in the 5th: Boldly showing others your creative side.

Pisces in the 9th: Surrendering to a belief or guiding principle.

The last birth chart bit is aspects. Aspects to your Persephone tell of the dialogues in your psyche she's engaged in with other energies in your consciousness. Conjunctions indicate merging, sextiles trigger and stimulate, squares apply friction and pressure needing release, trines support and boost, and oppositions confront and challenge to face-offs.

The Ceres-Persephone Dialogue

For kicks: Understanding the dialogue between your Ceres (asteroid 1) and Persephone will also shed light on how your internal wiring related to this story is configured. The statement that Ceres makes is one of protection of others, sometimes at the expense of risking living a rich, full life. The statement that Persephone makes is of wanting to be launched into new ways of being, those that provide her with opportunities to function as her own agent and thereby live with and from a greater feeling of wholeness, but not knowing how to make it happen. Look at the symbolism of each asteroid in your natal chart to uncover a new level of dialogue between these two parts of you, even if they're not in aspecting each other. Hint: Your Ceres is where you might look after others before yourself, and your Persephone is where you might hope someone else might show you how to become self-determined.

Persephone's Ransom

What will it take for Ceres to get her Persephone back? What does her freedom from Hades cost? Ceres doesn't stop until she gets Persephone back for two-thirds of the year, while her daughter is to spend only a third of the year with her husband. Ceres perceives she feels satisfaction from having Persephone back in her fold (she allows the crops and plants of the earth to bloom again), yet Persephone will never again be the perfect daughter. The young one has been initiated into an adult way of living and can never go back, can never retreat to the innocent time when she did not know herself as an adult and had no idea how to take responsibility for herself.

Because she can never recapture the sense of not knowing how important to a healthy sense of individuality are self-responsibility, self-determine and self-care, it turns our there's no ransom. She's moved on. Persephone's already grown up.

Chiron: Difference, Resourcefulness, and Mastery

We often hear about Chiron as the wounded healer, but there's so much more to this myth. I consider Chiron central to the transition from the Piscean Age to the Aquarian Age that's just beginning, in fact.

After his birth, his mother rejects him. When he was conceived, she was in the form of a horse. She had taken that form because Kronos, who saw her and just had to have her, was chasing her and she thought to outrun him. He also took the form of a horse and caught up to her, forcing himself on her.

When little Chiron was born, his mother Philyria was back to her humanoid form. He was born as a centaur, half-horse and half-human. She was not at all expecting this and was horrified. Her basic reaction was, "Get this monster away from me!"

He was given over to Apollo and Diana to be raised. They taught him all they knew (the healing and martial arts among them) and he became competent in a number of areas of study. As an adult, he taught many of these and other arts. He so good at what he did, he was the go-to teacher when heroes were preparing for their quests.

Chiron was different from the other centaurs, who were born wild. The others were born from centaur parents, and carried on in ways far from the civilized attitudes imparted to Chiron by Apollo and Diana. There are many stories of drunkenness and brawls resulting from their gathering together, including ruining weddings and accidental deaths. The rest of the centaurs didn't accept him, and neither did humans. He was left to live on the fringes of society.

He chose to create meaningful life, filling it with studies and, eventually, teaching others what he knew. Chiron was renowned for his resourcefulness in many areas of study and life, and was considered masterful at all he chose to undertake.

I see Chiron as a sensitizer to energetic information, which includes emotions. Our Chirons serve as antennas for energy around us, and what we do with it is entirely up to us. When we learn to manage that antenna, we can use this sensitivity for wonderful things. With it, we can feel into what's going on in people around us and can be uniquely positioned to work with others in ways and on levels that regular dealings and conversation simply can't enable.

How We Live Chiron Stories

These three sections can be taken on their own or seen as a process of evolving along the Chiron archetype.

Difference

A major way Chiron shows up in our birth charts and lives is to show in what ways we feel ourselves to be different from others. By house, sign and aspect, our Chiron placements reveal in what arena of life we expect to be treated as different. It tells us where we expect to be rejected just for being who we are.

The energy is in us from birth. In each of us it is activated in infancy, when a parent or other primary caregiver seems to reject us for doing something we are naturally wired to do. Since parents/caregivers are God/Goddess (everything comes to us from them and they are therefore everything to us), we can't let them be wrong. We can't conceive of the notion they might be. We decide that if a parent thinks something about us is unacceptable, there must be something wrong with us. We then go about trying to suppress or edit this part of ourselves out, and then still experiencing rejection while thinking that we probably deserve it. I can't tell you how many fully-functioning, mature, and respectable adults are running around with this expectation of rejection imprinted on an inner infant. This is so prevalent in people that working through these issues forms a core of the astrological and spiritual counseling I do in my practice. People can spend years in therapy talking about an issue or meditating to try to work through an issue, with no results. The emotional imprint on an inner infant is often the source of the issue in these situations.

What we do as we experience that rejection years later determines our overall experience of the Chiron archetype. When we feel left out of some group for any reason, do we decide it means something about us? Do we internalize the rejection and think something must be wrong with us? Do we feel sorry for ourselves? Or do we move on, living our own lives anyway? When rejected by an individual, whether it be after a job interview, or in a dating or romantic or any other situation, do we decide that something's wrong with us? Or do we understand that we're not for that person and move on?

The law of attraction states that people and groups that reject you are not right for you where you are in your journey. It can hurt to be told you don't belong. Hold the intention that you are going to experience what's in your highest good, and you'll be rejected by all the right people at the right times. (And you'll be accepted by all the right ones at the right times, too.) There are also times when we experience rejection and it is reflecting to us that we reject a part of ourselves, probably the inner infant who needs the love and attention she perceives she didn't get from her parents.

In all the ways we are different, we have the opportunity to become empowered by accepting the fact that we are individuals and simply don't appeal to everyone. The reasons just do not matter. It's a simple fact that not everyone is for everyone else. How attuned we are to this truth has much to do with our karma, our Chiron configurations, and what we are taught by our families of origin about what it means to be different. And how willing we are to accept ourselves in all the ways that others do not can make all the difference in healing Chiron-related wounding.

Resourcefulness

Another area affected by Chiron in our lives is resourcefulness. If we can get past the emotional sting of the rejection that Chiron energy can bring regarding the ways in which we're different, we can learn to see in what ways our Chiron brings understanding into the subtleties of a part of life. This is the territory of the wounded healer, when a person can help others with the wound he or she has specifically because he or she knows a lot about it.

This is the second stage of Chironic evolution. To get to it in healthy ways, we learn to have compassion for ourselves. We absolutely cannot help others with the same pain of rejection as us without it. Sometimes, we get somewhere that looks like compassion, but we got there in less than healthy ways. We develop instead feeling and behavior complexes that are rooted in something more like pity and martyrdom. If this happens, we can seem to be helping others when we're actually bringing them down with us, maintaining a low level of vibration of pain from Chironic rejection and wounding. For someone in this situation, compassion is key. Such a person must go deep within in the spirit of healing and choose compassion for the self.

What happens in these kinds of stories is that while not fully processed with one's own wounding, one begins to attempt to help others. Like attracts like, and there is generated an atmosphere of suffering between people that reinforces the wounding of each. What Caroline Myss calls "woundology" results. Woundology is when we define ourselves in terms of our painful experiences. We are survivors of abuse, we are addicts or recovering addicts, we are victims of genocide or fraud or anything else that has hurt us. When we slip into such a frame of mind (no matter the original painful event or circumstance) we lock into place the identity of being someone who has been hurt. We can cease to see ourselves as dynamic individuals capable of, and empowered to create, change in our lives. We can sacrifice our power to our history, creating an identity out of a sense of defeat and powerlessness. Natural law dictates that whatever's happening in our energetic bodies will manifest in our physical bodies, and so these kinds of dynamics of powerlessness invariably create various sorts of health imbalances and illness.

This is just one way that many can go. Those who do not can tap into the resourcefulness they possess because of their grasp of energetic subtleties. Being able to feel into situations and understand the subtleties of interactions and the ways that people are wired can translate into interesting sorts of creativity that can find solutions to many persistent problems. This kind of resourcefulness finds its way through problems and, if necessary, around them. For one who trusts his or her Chironic sensitivity, this can be a wonderful gift to give the self and others.

Mastery

A third Chironic area in our life stories has to do with mastery. Once we get beyond giving meaning to the sting of rejection and move into helping others with the same wound, we have the opportunity to move into this stage.

I see Chironic mastery as grasping the spiritual truths behind the realities of suffering. At this point we've gone beyond identifying as wounded, and then (if healthy) progressed into helping other people accept themselves and learn to heal themselves. But we've also progressed beyond identifying as the wounded healer. Doing this and understanding the nature of suffering can lead one into seeing the spiritual truths behind suffering.

In those I've witnessed go through this process, I've seen a change that comes as close to personal, inner alchemy as I have imagined possible. It involves living from within the heart, which I call living a heart-centered life. The world is now experienced via an open heart. A person identifies as a spiritual being, and the realities of human experience are faced openly and with consciousness. Pain and suffering are not turned away from or feared, but are accepted as invitations to respond with deeper levels of compassion.

Relating as a spiritual self to the spiritual selves in others is a good summary of the state of Chironic mastery.

Summary

Our collective understanding of the Chiron archetype has been evolving for a mere 33 years. Evolving beyond identities as wounded and as healers, we can come into a spiritual maturity unprecedented on this planet.

Who do you want to be? Do you want to be a product of your history, the sum of your experiences, defined in terms of your past hurts? Or do you want to be a spiritual being having a human experience?

Either way, Chiron will help you gain a vocabulary for ways of being going forward.

Lucifer: For the Love of God

For this month's "Living Myth," I invite you to leave everything you've learned about the story of this fallen angel at the door. Myth is always used to instruct members of society about acceptable modes of thought and behavior, and Lucifer's story has been a key in Judeo-Christian social instruction to show us a set of attitudes and behaviors that are not socially acceptable.

You've heard that his story is about evil, and while it is, the definition of evil needs to get a reality check. Much cultural energy has been expended to keep you from connecting in a healthy way with the Lucifer part of you, the doubter and rebel. And yet it is a part of you, as is every archetype. You'll see here that more than about evil, the core of Lucifer's story is about service from a deep sense of devotion, and a story of bringing one's gifts (ahem, *light bearer* is what Lucifer means) to the world.

First Things First: Evil, Defined

Evil is moving away from what we know is good.

Period.

Each of us has an internal goodness barometer. Conceptions of what is good can vary from person to person and are informed by many factors, all flowing out from our specific cornucopias of social, religious and familial conditioning. When we move toward what we know is good, we're serving what we might capitalize as The Good. When we move away from what we know is good, we are in the energy of evil. Evil, then, is a separation from what we innately know is goodness (which of course can be thought of as God but doesn't have to be).

Personifying evil in the form of a/the devil is intended to keep you fearful of connecting meaningfully with this part of yourself. It is to keep you fearful of your true nature, in essence to keep you from loving yourself if you doubt what the mainstream is up to.

Mythology: The Hebrew Samael

We've all heard the Christian story of Lucifer, the fallen angel, even if we are not now and never were moving in Christian circles. Yet it's the earlier Hebrew version of the story that takes us into the heart of what's going on with this character.

According to the Judeo-Christian religion, on the 6th day, God creates man. God then asks all the angels to honor man by bowing down to him. The Archangel Michael does so immediately, but the Archangel Samael does not. Samael objects, saying that since the angels were created from and reflect God's divine essence, to bow down before a being made from dust is problematic. He means that it transgresses the logic God has used up to this point about the nature of God and just what is happening with all this creation business. Samael sees it not so much as a personal or class affront, but as a potential pointer to a lack of integrity on the part of God.

God hears Samael's complaint and doesn't agree, saying that a human is above all else in creation except for God himself. In Samael's mind, this proves that God's agenda has shifted and that something huge is absolutely and totally out of whack. He chooses to leave God's environs, and the third of the angels who happen to agree with him decide to tag along.

How We Live the Story

When this story gets co-opted by Christianity and Samael becomes Lucifer, it is here that he is vilified because he chooses to work *against* God. So, you might automatically assume that anyone living a Lucifer story is evil – a thief, wife beater, child molester, killer or any other heinous label (but you were supposed to leave those assumptions at the door!). Again, assuming that this archetype is about what we currently call evil is a misunderstanding.

Those of us who live a Samael/Lucifer story are living a story of doubt and dissent as a form of service. We're doubting the mainstream opinion or edict, whatever it may be, and dissenting, and perhaps withdrawing from the mainstream. We've confronted the mainstream idea or intention and our intellects have pointed out an error in logic or planning that we can see presents a serious moral problem, even as others might not see it, or might not agree with us.

What's not obvious is that Samael's departure from God's ranks is not because of his pride (the big warning against being Lucifer-like is that we'll be overly proud), but because of his commitment to serving God. He's using God's logic and perceives God to be out of integrity, and can't stay in God's environs in good faith and support the new, shiny, obviously morally-bankrupt agenda. His deepest desire is to serve God, but God's dearth of integrity in the moment inspires him to withdraw his support in order to continue to have integrity, almost as if for the both of them.

His rebellion and departure are acts of love. Samael's not willing to support God in doing something he knows God knows isn't right. When we live a Samael/Lucifer story, we sometimes have to rebel in order to make a point. We sometimes feel we must leave a place we love and in which we're valued, when those in charge steer the group or place into territory we cannot support entering.

Bringing the voice of doubt to God is a form of service to God and all of creation. And even as we have put ourselves apart, we still desire to serve.

Remaining apart from the situation is also a form of service, offering a reminder to the group and leader of the integrity perceived to have disintegrated. We make a statement with our rebellion that the leader or group as a whole is better if he/she/it remembers something critical that its actions say has been forgotten, and we are going to hold space as a reminder for it.

We've been trained to avoid as much as possible expressing our doubts about the integrity of the hegemony of wherever we are. There are many of us sufficiently Uranian to have not allowed cementing of or to have unlearned our Saturnian training to being good little members of society. And yet when you understand the truth of Samael's/Lucifer's story, you can come to see the difference between two groups of rebels: Those with causes and those without them. Being revolutionary with a heart full of a desire to serve the greater good is living a Samael/Lucifer story, while rebelling for the sake of rebellion, or mere change, or destruction is not.

Lucifer, Astrologically
Lucifer is asteroid number 1930. Where it falls in your chart is where the voice of doubt manifests in your life. It says that if you were to fully develop this energy in you, you would surely be overly proud, arrogant, self-serving and – here it is – evil. It is

simultaneously where, when you come to understand the use of that voice as a check on your motivations, you can develop and offer your greatest gifts to the world, to the good, to God – pick your own outer reality you find worthy of serving. The symbolism of your Lucifer configuration (by house, sign & aspect) tells you what you most doubt doing yet where you can turn that doubt into service, which is bringing your light into the world.

I know a woman with Lucifer conjunct her Pisces Sun in the 10th house, and conjunct the Midheaven. A graphic designer, she's very good at what she does. It took her a long time to get used to receiving praise for her work, because Lucifer on her 10th house Sun was manifesting as a voice of doubt that she should be receiving positive attention for being who she is in the world.

Another woman, with Lucifer in Capricorn in the 1st house, possesses a great deal of latent leadership qualities (also with Saturn in the 1st), yet she doubts that she should offer them. She is at times not sure she should take steps to express the kind of (strong-willed) person that she is. When I worked with her, she was employed by a family business that had become unhealthy for her to be a part of, and knew that she had to learn to trust herself more in order to move on.

The Antidote to Pride

Lucifer, after all, is Latin for "bearer of light." This energy in each of us is proud of the frankly super gifts we can offer others and the world. It does tell of an area of life in which we can become overly self-indulgent or prideful, as this gift we have to offer can make us feel extremely important as we give it, perhaps even Godlike. The antidote to self-aggrandizement and the like is in allowing our Lucifer to function as the voice of doubt while we check in with our hearts to ensure our motivations are where we'd like them to be. If we decide and act from our minds, Lucifer's domain (it is a mental energy), we decide and act out of a disconnection to our whole being. If we allow our Lucifer his input yet decide and act from our hearts, our actions will always come from a place we can respect, and his voice can help us make sure we're headed in the right direction for the right reasons.

For the Love of God

If you buy the Lucifer story about rebellion that paints this story as one of petty selfishness and base motivations (the standard telling), you might see Lucifer about anything *but* love. The truth is that his bottom line is service to God and all of creation. Everything he does he does from and for his love of God, showing us that rebellion and resistance is one form of service that we might be called to offer individuals, groups and situations in our lives about whom and which we care the most.

Lilith's Rage and Re-writing History

A couple of years ago I offered a Lilith workshop in Los Angeles. I walked the attendees through the nine stages of the archetype as I see them. I remarked that rage is only one stage of the archetypal journey (#5), yet we've been imprinted culturally to believe that it's the end of Lilith's journey – it's where Lilith *always* lands, *has* to land. As a result, our understanding of what it means to live her story is limited, leading to an anemic ability to imagine and understand what she means to us.

My work with Lilith is geared to reframe the dialogue on this archetype of the natural, wild feminine. Each time I work with a client and each time one of them reads the natal true Black Moon Lilith report I offer, it's reflected that I'm re-imaging Lilith for them. *Re-imagining her*, but perhaps more accurately, showing them how *they* can re-imagine their lives-as-Lilith in ways that honor who they really are, that show them it's okay to love themselves for being who they are, even if others haven't. We have been taught to fear the wild feminine, and to hate ourselves if it shows up in and as us. I've decided that it's time to dip into some historical revision, if history is the story of what happened as told by the people who won the battles.

As I often retell Lilith's story, I'm planting seeds in clients and readers that it's okay to love themselves for at times being Lilith, for bringing her themes to their families, professions, relationships and, in general, to the world. It's time for us to accept this part of ourselves that's been forced into shadow, that's been shoved deep down inside us and is, in some, rotting us from the inside out. Acceptance involves several steps, and one of the first is to admit into consciousness and acknowledge our feelings about being suppressed, or having been confronted with attempts to dominate us, and our responses to those attempts. Whether we acquiesced into despising ourselves or fled in rebellion, choosing to have freedom at all costs and losing our connection to a people and place to which we know belong does not matter. The important part is to learn to deal with the emotional imprints left on us from those experiences.

Which leads us to the rage for which Lilith is, and we-as-Lilith can be, famous. This chapter is the first in a series of four to work out issues along the archetypal journey we travel as we live Lilith's story as our own, cracking open the prevailing assumptions to show you how to connect with this part of you in new, self-loving ways.

History

According to the victors, the archetype of Lilith is about rage. If you're going to live a Lilith story, the prevailing line goes, it's going to be destructive and you're going to have to pay for it. If you bring her darkness to the world, we as the misinformed and maladapted group mind repeat to our young girls, you will be punished for it. We're to believe that pain, abuse, rape, diminishment, forced flight and abandonment are the natural consequences of knowing ourselves as Lilith, of admitting our connection to the natural, instinctive wild, and of being true to ourselves at all costs.

We have to a great degree accepted this, some of us more than others, having few to no models of healthy Lilith expression. Readers of The Mists of Avalon and other such works who long for the olden days of connection to nature and the Goddess in all her forms buy the prevailing story less than most, and sometimes that longing is rooted in deep personal (karmic) memories of times on earth when the wild feminine was acknowledged and honored, and not destroyed and ignored, not manipulated into turning on itself, not demonized, not pushed out of consciousness as much as is possible.

We have been told that rage is the outcome and the point of Lilith's story. This is a lie. Precisely because we as a (patriarchy-based) collective don't know how to deal with rage, and the deep pain that inspires it, we get stuck in our archetypal journeys as Lilith. In other words, because we as a collective no longer know how to deal with rage and the deepest pain, we tell each other there's no solution, no resolution to her story.

Critical to remember always, not just when thinking about Lilith, is that all rage is rooted in pain. The diminishment of the feminine hurts, and our forgetting of how to deal with it leads us to not know how to move beyond the stage in Lilith's journey that has to do with rage.

This misunderstanding of Lilith's story reflects a collective imbalance, a disconnection from the natural wild as it exists in ourselves and in the world around us. We fear the wild, we vilify nature, and we do what we can to introduce control and controlling ways of being so that no deviation from the mainstream, brain-based agenda may disrupt the status quo, what we are to believe is the well-oiled machine of our world, that of the patriarchy.

Here is a fact that is more obvious now than ever: *The patriarchal machine is well-oiled only when we sacrifice our connection to our true natures.* Its gears and axels are greased with our own individual, creative, wild, instinctive, passionate selves that we've offered in sacrifice to survive, or to prevent ourselves from making waves – sometimes willingly, sometimes not. The awareness of this fact is spreading like wildfire in the consciousnesses of individuals, as if the call to wake up to self-acceptance and self-love is an airborne virus too many of us too count are at present catching.

Re-writing History

Accepting the reality of the segments of your life as Lilith's story is the first step to re-writing your history. Opening to feel the depth and intensity of Lilith's pain, your pain for having been treated as a Lilith, is the next.

I have something to share with you that might sound more radical than my self-loving and -honoring approach to Lilith: *To learn what it is to be spirit having a human experience on this planet/plane, we each sign up for everything that happens to us. We have asked for all the experiences that we have had.*

If you're in touch with your rage, simply take this in as an idea. Let it enter your consciousness, and see if you can check your reaction. You might not be done being angry for having been abused and mistreated as a Lilith figure, or angry at yourself for having gotten yourself in it or what you chose to do to get out of it. And if this is so, it's fine. You won't be able to move beyond rage until you're ready. And if you're not ready but are reading this book, know that you're on your way, and trust that the timing of all of this – everything – is perfect.

Re-writing history is in allowing the meaning we've assigned to our life events to alter. We do this after the introduction of self-responsibility for all that's happened and is happening now, and then opening to the next step, which is compassion.

We must accept that people who treat us negatively when we bring out Lilith are acting out the collective disconnection to the wild, the group fear of the wild. They are responsible for their behavior – and perhaps could use a few sessions with a compassionate evolutionary astrologer – and yet they are acting out something bigger than themselves. Compassion without accepting responsibility for our experiences leads to confusion, and I don't advocate letting everything go in order to be a peacemaker. But honoring yourself means taking responsibility for what's happened, loving yourself for being just who you are even if, and often specifically *because* you're Lilith, and forgiving others for not understanding how to gracefully accept you as a representative of the wild instinctive, for failing to honor you as you need to be honored.

In Real Life

My own Lilith is conjunct Neptune-Mercury-Moon in Sagittarius, in the 2nd with Mercury on the cusp of the

3rd and Moon in the 3rd. Writing and teaching about Lilith, and supporting you-as-her, is important to my own reconnection with the wild. Here's the major Lilith-related story of my own Mercurial/vocal suppression from my childhood: When I was around age 5, I wrote three four-letter words on a small chalkboard. I knew them, that was all. I knew that they were in category together, and I enjoyed words. I can't stop using words of all sorts, and my nature is not to judge them (I sometimes wonder how I survived the language-less state of infancy). I'm sure at other times I wrote the names of trees and animals, or foods and numbers. My father saw it when I was finished and flipped out! It was the only time in my childhood that he spanked me. I accept that he did what *he* thought was best, being very sensitive to language, linguistic conventions and the power of words (he worked as a radio DJ and had majored in speech in college), and wanted to strongly negatively reinforce the use of what he thought were inappropriate words, especially in a 5-yr old. I personally don't think that taking a kid over your knee is an appropriate solution, but I accept that he did what he thought was best, confronted by totally unacceptable language from his young child.

I have a client born the day after me, so our charts are in many ways similar. Her Neptune-Lilith-Mercury in Sagittarius are in the 3rd. Her first question to me was about what's trying to come through her. With this stellium in Sagittarius in the 3rd, we explored what it means for her to connect to Lilith within her and begin to bring the energy out in proactive ways. As with all Lilith-Mercury aspects (and underscored by the stellium being in the 3rd house, a house of Mercury), "doing" Lilith for her means letting herself think of and speak about Lilith's themes, and to communicate her feelings about having experienced suppression of her voice because other people feared the wild in her. I didn't ask about what happened in her childhood, but I'm confident that at least a few things she said when young made someone nervous and she was punished for it, learning quickly to edit out what might make others uncomfortable and bring on punishment.

I have every confidence that she will work through the memories of suppression and choose compassion for those who inspired it, and that she will be able to accept that her family and others who inspired her to put a lid on her mind and voice were doing what they thought was best for her. If we carry Lilith in our mind and voice, those who love us will do what they can to help us understand that society does not, generally speaking, welcome the influence of Lilith. Most of our families have absorbed the collective's fear of the wild, and when they see it in us, threatening to remove the lid of the ordered reality we need to survive, they will teach us to be quiet in whatever way they can.

We can't deny our memories of suppression, and we can't deny our deep pain at the long-term diminishment of the feminine. Compassion is a key part of coming out Lilith's rage, yet we need to be fully in touch with our feelings and take responsibility for our experiences in order to do so. The level of emotional healing represented by addressing our cache of Lilith experiences is needed by many at this time, and you're not alone in your suspicion that it's a good thing for you to accept and love yourself for who you are. Once we've begun healing the suppression of instinct our Lilith represents, we can begin to integrate what she has to say into our lives healthy, positive, and proactive ways.

Lilith's Flight

In this second installment of Lilith's myth as we live it, our focus is on Lilith's departure from home in order to maintain her autonomy.

The Story
Back to Genesis and commentaries on it from the Hebrew tradition: God creates Adam male and female. After a while, Adam realizes and tells God that he's lonely – every *other* animal has a mate but him. God splits Adam into two, male and female – Adam and Lilith. Adam's happy because he has someone to play with, right? Right. Well...sort of. Okay, *yes*, except that she won't do what he says. She insists on being treated as an equal, since they were made at the same time of the same stuff. When it's clear that Adam will have none of this equality business, she splits. She heads off to the edge of the Red Sea and plays with the spirits who congregate there, enjoying herself, enjoying her (pro-) creativity.

Can You Put Up With Inequality?
A better question is, Do you choose to put up with it? Not everyone living Lilith stories splits. Not everyone heads out the door for some glorious, imagined future. It involves stepping out into the great unknown, and

either trusting life and the universe that you're taken care of or, perhaps more often, trusting that your instincts will get you by. And then still others of us don't trust anything, we just head out because anything's better than de facto slavery.

Leaving Home Stinks

For those of us who do leave, I can't emphasize enough the importance of processing the feelings engendered by leaving the place in/to which you know you belong. Lilith's natural other half is Adam, and leaving the situation is extremely difficult. It's her home. It's where she belongs, where she knows she belongs. It's not that Adam's her home, but that the place they create together and share is.

The tension that arises in a person facing the prospect of being dominated or flinging the self out into the great unknown needs resolution. There are of course times when leaving is the only answer. They are when we are threatened with violence, and when power plays develop as others attempt to control us, to make us into some kind of manageable version of human that is, in fact, a little less than human.

When I tell Lilith's story, I make her destination sound great. She's free!, I say, free to do as she pleases! She's left the dull-witted would-be oppressor and creates freedom for herself, finds great and appropriate outlets for expressing her true nature, and an authentic connection to her sexual nature! And then I remind people how difficult it is to leave the place you know you belong in, and to. It's not to play a trick. I do this because when in bad Lilith-related situations, we glorify freedom, and we can't imagine how hard it will actually be to leave what we've known as our true home. Honest work with your Lilith chart configuration and history needs to acknowledge that there are times when both options can cause us pain. We have to know what we're getting into if we're going to make such a major change. Stepping into these situations with our eyes less than fully open is what gets us caches of unresolved emotional debris, the processing and release of which is the point of my work with Lilith, with you-as-Lilith.

But wait a minute – do we really have to leave? In all sorts of relationships we face moments that seem forks in our roads. A trick is to learn to distinguish between what are and what are not threats to our autonomy, attempts to in some way lord over or enslave us. Those of us with histories of living Lilith's stories, or certain brands of negative Aries, Virgo, Libra, Scorpio, or Pisces stories for that matter, might exhibit knee-jerk reactions against anything that even remotely appears to fence us in.

Whether we leave or stay, in any given situation in our lives that resonates with Lilith's departure from Adam, there might be stuff left over to process.

If We Left

We might carry pain from choosing to cut ourselves off from home, where we know we belong. Even when it stinks, is painful, brings us to know abuse and violence, home can still be comforting. We tend to stick to what's familiar, and removing from our lives a giant chunk of it called "home," stepping out into the proverbial wilderness of the world, can be difficult. If we left, we might carry a rootlessness, a restlessness because what we felt was home is no longer an option for us, and no longer welcomes us.

What feels like home will change. Perhaps it is a family-of-origin home we chose to leave, perhaps the home we made with a first love. Whatever the home it was, the necessity of our departure automatically contributes to a revision of what an appropriate home is. Home will never be home again, while at the same time we learn new ways of and reasons for creating a home. I suspect that many people living Lilith stories learn how to make their home wherever they happen to be, as their relationship with self can be strengthened incalculably by honoring self enough to step out of a bad situation to make a better one somewhere else, even if no particulars can be imagined at the time of departure.

If We Stayed

Perhaps we realized that we weren't in truth as threatened as we at first felt. Perhaps our mates, partners and parents opened to listen to us, and to honor our need for autonomy after all. Or, perhaps we stepped back from the great unknown of the proverbial wilderness of the world (please tell me if I'm not using enough clichés), weren't ready to step into the unknown. Or maybe we chose not to stand up for ourselves after all. If this is the case (and I can tell you that at some point in the life of those of us living Lilith stories we did not), the work is in (if you're not in immediate danger now) forgiving yourself for stepping back from the edge, for choosing not to venture out into the great unknown.

There is nothing more damaging than self-hate. The hate of others in no way compares, and we open the door for them to hate us if we hate ourselves. We can no longer afford to cycle through the Piscean Age control-based political, philosophical and religious doctrines that were devised to keep us from knowing and loving ourselves. They were created to keep us from being able to see the wonderful being each of us is. If you didn't leave, and you in some way regret it, or wonder what it would have been like if you'd left, accept that it was what you were ready for at that time. It fit your journey, you needed to see more of the situation, you needed to choose one more time to stay where it wasn't good, but it was at least familiar...

And now you know more than you did then. If you encounter the power plays again, you'll know better what to do. I like to invite people to see how to make choices from a place of self-love, to ask themselves which option makes their hearts expand and which makes them contract. Which potential result brings them more alive, and which seems to take life out of them? When phrased that way, it makes everything seem so simple, doesn't it? The reality is that choosing new behaviors and breaking habits isn't easy, especially when we're talking the protection rackets we've manufactured in our psyches to make sure we avoid repeating the kind of deep emotional pain Lilith-as-us can carry. And yet we all have choice in each moment, and we are all exploring just what it is to be incarnated on earth, spirit having a human experience, one relationship, experience and choice at a time.

Lilith and Seduction

If you want to get behind what any mythic story really has to offer, start with the stereotypes associated with it. See how they tell of real choices people have made about living the archetypal energy. See that they're possibilities available to us, and get clear that that's all they are. In any given culture, there are sets of acceptable and unacceptable behaviors that are communicated to the masses by the myths/stories it tells. Sometimes it's tough to live an archetypal story that differs from the culturally shaped myth we think we're living, and easier to believe that the only option to how the story turns out is how we're told the mythic figure lived it. And yet our archetypal experiences can differ greatly from the myths we've had ingrained in us. This chapter looks at one of the stereotypes associated with Lilith, seduction.

Stereotypes: Socio-Psychic Memes and Expectations
(How's that for a heading?)

A major facet of Lilith's story as we've received it as social instruction is that sexual freedom is dangerous. Such freedom has often been labeled promiscuity, and numerous negative labels applied to those (usually women) who explore their sexual selves with others. Practical issues aside (potential disease and unwanted pregnancy, etc.), the root of this is that if a woman chooses her own sexual partners, she will likely confound the choice of husband her family might have in mind for her. If this sounds outdated to you, remember that the inner threads of a culture's fabric change slowly over time, and here we're looking at the underlying thoughts and assumptions about what a story means.

If a woman is empowered to choose her sexual partners, the patriarchal system of inheriting property is thrown out of whack. The political, business and social allegiances formed through marriage have been an integral part of the development of many human cultures for many thousands of years. The last few decades have seen a rise in Western cultures of a need to recognize the fact of equality between the sexes, yet it wasn't that long ago that these ideas were dangerous to the established order. Keep in mind as you read this that there are many place on Earth where nothing's changed for many thousands of years; where women are treated as property to seal business, political and family alliances. Their virginity is treated as a prize, the most important part of the deal – the most important thing about them.

Lilith's sexuality is seen as dangerous by Adam, her natural other half, her rightful mate. Once they're split by the deity from the one being both male and female into the two that are one of each, there's some rub. Adam expects her to be subservient to him, and she lets him know they're equals. His take is that she's somehow less, and that his desire to always be on top during their lovemaking inspires her to leave him: Better to be anywhere else than a slave.

After she leaves, it's said she goes to the edge of the Red Sea and copulates at will (but we're to read into this that she does this "a ton/way too much") with the demons who reside there. I think of these demons as beings, souls, energies, who live there. They're beings other than Adam but most importantly, beings outside the control of Adam's god. Yet in the mythology, which is social instruction, these others must be described as demonic. We're supposed to look down on her choice to have freedom and be personally (which includes sexually) expressive, and become afraid to make the same choice. She's said to be a harlot, a whore, and if you're a woman and you pick your own partners for your own reasons, the old meme goes, then you are too.

Shame as Currency

Our culture is built upon the repression of natural sexuality. Who gets to bed whom when is a foundation of this property system we're living in the shadow of. Even as many individuals' choices are no longer officially regulated by the old patriarchal interest in marriage, many of us do feel a lingering shame about making our own choices regarding our sexuality if those choices fall outside the bounds of traditional expectations.

Now, perhaps most people drawn to this book have nothing to do with such conventions, whether raised outside them or having wised up and *no thank you*-ed the toxic sludge being handed you by family, school, religion and others. But those in the latter category might have retained bits of it, just from past exposure to it.

How guilty a person feels about his or her natural choices is a form of cultural capital, or currency, that one needs to feel at home in this type of culture. On some level, our society can seem held together by the secret shame people have about their natural inclinations. Healthy human sexuality includes operating outside the consensus norms at least sometimes, and learning to be a little more like Lilith, unashamed of her recognition that she's an animal, connected to nature and all that means. Adopting her attitudes could help many of us learn about what real health and balance in our lives looks like.

This is the time to get to the bottom of whatever you're carrying about this stuff. Pluto's entrance into Capricorn in early 2008 asked us to unearth who's really in charge of us, and as Capricorn's the sign of authority & conditioning, this includes what we were taught when young about how and how not to be.

Whether we listened or not, we absorbed at least some of it. It's time to unearth it and let it go.

Sex As Power

And all of the above just to get here. It's necessary, as looking at the reality of how we live Lilith's stories straight on requires us to dig some.

When we feel on the wrong side of power, we can be inspired to use whatever tools to which we have access to get some power back. Or, perhaps, our survival is at stake and we reach into our repertory for whatever can help us stay alive, and that might be our bodies themselves. Our history of using sex and sexuality as a means to control behavior and gain power over each other has resulted in a great majority of us at some point in many of our lives using sex to gain power. The power to seduce another, to entice another to give in to the urges of the chemical-infused & visceral animal nature, can seem to eliminate the power gap. It can reveal those in radically different social strata as ultimately the same.

As I write this, the Sun is just a few days into Scorpio. I've been thinking about Scorpio the last few days as a result, watching the Sun begin to shine a light on issues of power and control. Scorpio is a sign closely related to Lilith's journey, given the experience of the Lilith archetype in exploring the right to have personal autonomy yet still have intimate others in close proximity, as long as they're the right ones and for the right reasons. Scorpio gone wrong is the basis of our thoughts and expectations about it: Drama, power plays, abuse, backstabbing, betrayal. These reflect a misunderstanding of Scorpio, however: True power isn't to be found by controlling other people, it's only found via truly knowing, accepting, and controlling the self.

This applies to the healing and learning invitations associated with Lilith-related seduction. Sex as power over others never yields power – *never*. It results in a temporary perception of having gained the upper hand. What results are the famous Scorpionic webs some of us thoughtlessly slip into and then spend half our lives trying to figure out how to get out of. The real juice of Scorpio and Lilith, the only place where power surrounding sexuality can be found, is in being in touch with one's deepest reality and sense of self, and *then* making choices based in that self-knowledge.

Whatever You Chose

Are you someone who's used sex to gain power, or felt the victim of sexual power dynamics? Or are you someone who's been afraid of sex because of the power dynamics/nonsense it seems to stir? Either way, there's some work for you to do. Access to and expression of our sexual selves is vital to health and sanity.

Healing choices for the present require deep self-knowing. What you think and feel about sex, and yourself as a sexual being, is ready to be seen or revisited if you're drawn to this book. It might seem counterintuitive, but sexual healing begins with you as an individual. Here are some steps to stir the process, if it's time for you to begin.

(Oh, but first, if there's any confusion in you about the difference between sex and love, stop having sex with others and learn what it means to love yourself. Loving yourself first is the key to learning to choose the right kinds of relationships and situations for yourself, to stop the Scorpionic web patterns mentioned above.)

1. Understand the reasons behind your choices in the past (both recent and distant) is where to start. Get behind what you might have thought you were doing/getting to what you can see now you really learned. There's no doubt that sometimes our most important lessons are painful.
2. Accept your choices as necessary to your unfolding path. You incarnated on Earth to have the experience of exploring what it means to be soul embodied in one of these human vehicles, and everything you've experienced is integral to that exploration.

3. Let go of what you believe your past choices meant about you. Release the comments and judgments of others you might have internalized, whether in their words or how they looked at and treated you (or didn't). See each of those experiences as showing something about yourself to support you in getting to a place of deeper self-knowing.
4. Look at where you are today. Gauge what you feel right *now*, in *this* moment. Get in touch with who you are and what is the right way for you to live *in this moment*. If you take the time to truly explore this side of yourself, you'll be stepping into a place of self-love. And it is this place from which you should make all choices in your life not just about sex, but about everything.
5. Whatever choices you make now, make them because they resonate with who you know you are. Your heart (4th chakra, in the middle of your chest) will open when something resonates with you, and close when something doesn't. It is a simple circuit (open or closed) that can tell us in any moment if we're headed in the direction of self-love or somewhere else.

Reconciling Adam and Lilith

In my ongoing work with the Lilith archetype, my basic goal is to re-imagine how her story as we live it can turn out. If you've been keeping up with my work, you know that I'm supporting people in imagining for themselves how their version of her story turns out, as it doesn't have to end painfully and tragically as the culture seems to insist. Again, myths are tools for social instruction, examples we provide each other about how to be productive members of society. We use myths to ensure that people know what are acceptable and unacceptable attitudes and behaviors. Of course we do, right? Isn't it a society's job to make sure its members know what to do and not do?

As the cultural line on Lilith has been that she's not acceptable, or that she's acceptable only if she's willing to be demonized and exist in little-discussed fringes of the fold, we've inherited the instruction that we shouldn't be like her. It says that we shouldn't stand up for ourselves. We shouldn't assert, expect or – heaven forbid! – demand equality. We shouldn't honor our instinctive wisdom over what we're told is happening. We learn when we do bring her out (when outside the little-discussed fringes of the fold) that we won't be accepted.

Now that we've looked at Lilith's rage, flight and seduction, it's time to look at how to reconcile these two natural mates in our lives as we live the stories.

Other Halves

If you know Lilith's story from most existing sources, chances are you've got it in your head that the split between Lilith and Adam is permanent, and needs to be. He's a just going about his business like any regular dude and she's a nasty, psychotic woman who has to get away from him, that version of the story goes. She demands equality but doesn't pull her weight, he demands total control and doesn't even know who she is.

But let's start with the fact that each is the other's natural other half. In the Judeo-Christian mythos, they were created at the same time and from the same stuff. In Genesis, God created Adam male and female. After the animals were named, Adam told God of his loneliness, so God split Adam into male and female, like all the other animals who had mates – natural other halves. As far as I'm concerned, when honest with themselves, they crave one another. They're two halves of one being. They belong together, and they know it.

Sometimes regarding Lilith we hear that she can't be in relationship, or won't. This is only true if the relationship is categorically anything. Healthy Lilith wants to be in relationship, but only in those that allow her freedom to be exactly who she is. For some people with heavy Lilith signatures (whether male or female, gay or straight or somewhere between), this means not living with a mate or spouse. For some, it means no monogamy. For others, it means spending 67 happily married years with the same person under the same roof. Just as we have to allow that Lilith as we live her is complex and dynamic, there's no single way the relationship story with Lilith as we live her stories turns out.

Adam and Lilith long to be together. As it stands today (if they've been trained to be good members of Western society), they often have no idea how to do that. If you're Adam, living an upstanding, socially-acceptable life, there's a part of you that wants Lilith, the free and wild influence who brings the primal into your world. You know you have to have it – life is boring and halfway meaningless without it.

If you're Lilith, expressing your primal wisdom and living deeply into yourself as an extension of nature, there's a part of you that wants Adam, grounded into reality and reliable as he is…or *could* be. You know you have to have it – life boring and halfway meaningless without it.

Given these statements, it's time to look at just who Adam is.

But Who is This Adam?

The first thing to note is that we don't generally consider Adam to be a mythological figure. He underlies our (Western) cultures' conception of what it means to be a man, and this archetype is so deeply ingrained in how we conceive of ourselves and live, we don't see him that way. But he is. The success of a theology rests on the success of the mythologies used to support it, and Adam is definitely an archetypal figure whose stories many of us live in our daily lives.

Adam, as we've received his story implicitly through cultural channels, is the guy who does well because he does what God says. He's the model of upright behavior, and always knows his place in the grand scheme of things.

Adam's a yes-man. As long as he does what God tells him, everything's great. He can have power and position if he does. Being a yes-man dilutes not just your personal power, but your imagination, your zest for life…it dilutes *you*.

How can we live this archetype in better ways? A sense of personal honor and integrity is a must. You have to make sure that what you're adopting as honorable is actually honorable – and you have to use your own inner goodness barometer to know this and choose the right thing to do. (Playing at Adam in healthy ways requires learning to integrate Lucifer.)

We can live Adam in healthy ways also by implementing structure to our lives and the world around us while we never lose sight of the realities of human nature and needs. Too often, the control principle embodied by how we live Adam's story gets completely out of hand. An idea or vision, no matter how wonderful on paper, can get concretized via means and into forms that do injustice to how we live as humans. Or to make them work or perpetuate them, we seem to have to sacrifice something integral to our human natures (lifelong careers at huge businesses can do this, for example).

A healthy Adam also takes responsibility for his part in the world. The Judeo-Christian version of Adam that we've received says that as long as we do what God tells us to do, everything's great. Well, look at the state of the planet and the health of humanity that's resulted from running with Adam-related themes without a sense of responsibility! Doing Adam in healthy ways is entirely possible, but we have to take responsibility for our actions even as the traditions tell us we don't.

Along the Way
If you identify with the cultural line on Lilith and find Adam repugnant (men are pigs, etc.), you miss out on the stabilizing influence we can have on each other.

You shut out the energy of directedness and intentionality.

If you identify with the cultural line on Adam and find Lilith unacceptable, (women are inexplicable, crazy, etc.), you miss out on the enlivening influence we can have on each other. You shut out the energy of instinct and freedom.

In other words, you miss out on understanding both sides of yourself. Just as Adam was created male and female, so were you. Each of us has both sides to us. Learning to honor ourselves in our completeness (and then opening to play with others who do the same thing) is how we create total, utter, radical happiness.

Is there something about your natural other half that you don't like? Is there something about one half or the other inside you that you don't like? Living the Adam and Lilith myths in healthy ways calls us to reconcile our own Adams with our own Liliths.

What Does Reconciliation Require?

To get along and live together and be happy, Lilith must honor her true nature, and Adam must behave in honorable ways...and then they must honor each other. As we have received the story of Lilith, she's uncontrollable and vindictive, nasty and the sort of woman you don't want to be around. As we've received the story of Adam, he's bossy and doesn't settle for less than getting what he wants, which is to say total control and/or domination.

We have to learn to deflect the cultural memes with which we've been bombarded about what men and women are like. Many people have of course done this to free themselves up for living healthy lives, but have they made peace with their histories of being on one side of the fence or the other, given that the culture teaches us there's a war on?

Know your true inner self, know your needs. Know how you're wired, what it is that you want to experience in life, and who's welcome to come in and play with you. Know and then accept all of this, and then honor other people for who they are, and you're on your way to learning how Adam and Lilith can live together in total, utter, radical happiness.

Ariadne and Abandonment

As always, I aim to look at how our lives can be informed by stories we've inherited from the collective memory & consciousness. There are sometimes many versions or variations of a story, bringing the potential for many garden paths that seem tangential if we really get into a myth. But we have to understand that myths are always used by those running things to instruct members of the society about appropriate modes of behavior and belief. Each of these chapters steps into how we as individuals live at least a part of a mythic story, and how to navigate through it when we make choices from, let's say, not the most conscious or grounded of stances. Understanding how to learn to navigate these stories can open to a major avenue of growth.

Ariadne appears as an interesting one to me because it's been part of our collective storytelling for a long time, and also because there's a gold mine in it both as we live it and how we have re-imagined its themes in the last few decades through the lens of feminism.

The Story
On the island of Minos is a famous maze to which a group of young men annually is sent from Athens as a

sacrifice. In this particular year, a guy named Theseus is among them. He's not your regular sacrificial volunteer, though. In fact, he has volunteered to kill the Minotaur, the half man-half bull monster who lives in the maze. So, he's looking to be a hero. He goes to Minos with the intention of killing the monster for his own glory and that of his people.

Ariadne is the daughter of King Minos and half-sister to the Minotaur. It's said that at first sight she falls for Theseus, and desired to help him. She is said to give him a sword and thread, enabling him to find his way into the maze, kill the Minotaur, and find his way out again. He agrees to take her off the island (away from her cruel father, which she has wanted for a long time), and they set out. On the journey, she wakes up one day to find herself on the island of Naxos, left behind. Dionysus, the god who is a priest of the goddess and a lover of women, rescues and marries her.

Your classic stand-by-your-man-then-get-dumped-on-some-crummy-island-while-you're-sleeping story, right? She helps him get into and out of the dangerous labyrinth, enabling him to kill the Minotaur, which is his heroic quest and gift to his people...and then he unceremoniously leaves her behind while she sleeps. He doesn't even have the guts to *tell* her he's leaving her. What a jerk, right? Hold your judgments for a bit. This is one we have to look at with different eyes, the eyes we use to see our lives as brimming over with examples to see how we have free will, choice and, most importantly, responsibility for our circumstances and lives.

It might seem that since Ariadne doesn't know that Theseus is going to desert her, that when she helps him she's just doing what she thinks will help the man she loves. But she knows what she's doing. She's throwing herself into the hands of this man, leaving her fate up to him because how it's been going so far isn't that great. She wants a change in her life, and Theseus can offer it. The story as we live it is really about an expectation of reciprocity from another that is, at root, a betrayal of self. We give everything away and then feel lost because we have nothing left.

Why does Ariadne help Theseus? What does she hope to gain? What does she want?

Let's not forget that Theseus is pretty much a doomed man. Ariadne falls in love at first sight with a man sentenced to death. So, we have a story of a woman whose feelings fly in the face of the reality of the unfolding events in front of her. So it's a story about passion? Or maybe about true love?

How We Live Ariadne's Story
As Ariadne lives in us, she thinks that sacrifice is noble, and so she sacrifices herself. If you live her

story, look at the times another's choices about his or her life seemed a betrayal to you. The mindset that anyone else is responsible for you is a deep malfunction in our present conception of self. If you were betrayed, you had the door for betrayal open. You opened it. The trick is in being willing to see in what ways we're willing to lose ourselves, to abandon ourselves to another...for any reason.

It would be easy to imagine this archetype is about abandonment by others. It would be too simple, actually. Aren't we spiritually more mature than thinking what happens to us is because of others? As it happens, so far we *have* been that not mature. Yet the worst kind of betrayal is the betrayal of self. *We experience this in our relationships only when we do it to ourselves.* Our relationships mirror our inner workings. Welcome to the cusp of the transition to the Aquarian Age. Putting responsibility on others is *so* Piscean Age, people, and aren't you evolving out of the mass-control, everything-that-happens-is-someone-else's-responsibility, humans-are-supposed-to-be-sheep Piscean-Age mindset?

Ariadne as we live her story doesn't want to know that she is her own responsibility. *This horrible thing happened to me and look where it left me.*

Villains, Victims and Interpersonal Transactions

Since the 1970s and feminist re-readings and re-imaginings of our myths, it's tempting to make a villain out of Theseus. It can be attractive to put the blame for Ariadne's situation on him. What's absolutely crucial to understand is that Ariadne, as is each of us, is responsible for her circumstances. This is not "blaming the victim" but a case of understanding that blaming anyone else for our choices and their outcomes is the choice to avoid taking responsibility for ourselves. We're to think of her as a victim, and to think that she should be angry for being so treated.

We certainly can read this myth as worthy of inspiring male-bashing (or perhaps just Athenian-hero bashing). But the reading of the myth we've inherited has been massaged in such a way as to reinforce the cultural values of the day. And that's how we've lived it, but it's time to grow out of "cruel man leaves helpless girl because she cramps his style."

Something that complicates this story is that there are multiple transactions in their relationship.

1. Ariadne helps Theseus navigate the maze.
2. Theseus takes her off the island.

Each is a discrete happening. First, Ariadne helps Theseus, giving him the tools to win his quest, something he couldn't have done without such help. Second, Theseus takes her off the island, something she's wished for and wasn't able to do on her own.

We tend in our relationships to do something to get something, and yet we have to unlearn this. We have to remember that what's worth doing for another is worth *giving* to that other with no expectations of reciprocity. Whatever we do while expecting something in return will lead us to unhappiness but, more importantly, lead us out of self-responsibility and integrity.

As we live this story, reciprocity is expected. Reciprocity is a business arrangement, and is a technical feature of many of our relationships. But it is not a part of love. Love is from the part of us that wants to give, that exists to give. Does Ariadne give to Theseus out of love? Or does she give with the expectation of receiving a one-way ticket off Minos? I think we can imagine her stuck on the little island of Naxos, with no home and no other, and sure she's better off than at the mercy of her cruel father.

Why do we have to make her powerless or bereft because she was left behind on Naxos? Of course she needs to mourn the loss of both home and the budding relationship, but her choices have got her where she is. Which is far away from her cruel father, and a world of possibility thereby opened up to her. She wanted that for a long time, and she's finally got it. I think that's pretty empowering.

Wait, one more thing. What should we make of Dionysus rescuing and marrying her? After everything, Ariadne still possesses her true nature; her real self isn't ruined by the encounter with Theseus. We are supposed to expect her to be and remain damaged, but she isn't. It's her true self that Dionysus sees when he looks at her. He doesn't pity her, far from it. A priest of the Goddess and a lover of women doesn't let such a story of unfortunate happenings distract him from seeing the richness she is and possesses outside of one relationship that didn't work out well.

Living into spiritual maturity at this time involves retelling this story and understanding that no one's truly a victim. No one's really abandoned by others. Each and every one of us is magnificently powerful and is creating our lives as we go. Every time we feel abandoned by another, it's an opportunity to understand in what ways we have abandoned ourselves and let the image of being a victim take us over.

Arjunsuri
Finding Conscience on the Path to Truth

The phrase *Finding Conscience on the Path to Truth* encapsulates the journey we each at some point take related to the archetype of Arjunsuri, asteroid 20300. Whenever we seek to align ourselves with truth, whether a truth or Truth, we live out a piece of a process that's about learning if what we're aligning with is a right or appropriate thing for us to align with. A question that inspires and summarizes the journey, and one we have to answer as we go, is "Does what I serve serve me?"

This chapter introduces the mythology, archetype and archetypal journey of Arjunsuri, a new tool for astrologers to understand the experiences people have with their beliefs and truths as they seek to know what's true.

The Name
The name Arjunsuri is a composite of Arjuna, the protagonist in the most important Hindu religious text, the *Bhagavad Gita*, and Suri, an epithet for Krishna, the Hindu face of God figuring prominently in that text. The journey of the archetype culminates in embodiment of a teaching or agenda following a variously and deeply inquisitive process and living life

in a way externally reflecting the demands of one's conscience. At the end of the *Bhagavad Gita*, following his process of questioning, Arjuna embodies Krishna's teaching. The name of God is appended to Arjuna's name to reflect this embodiment; Arjuna becomes the instrument of Krishna when he lives out Krishna's teaching.

Arjuna's Story

In the *Bhagavad Gita*, one of the foundational texts of Hinduism, a warrior named Arjuna is called to take the field of battle against his cousins, who have been trying for years to eliminate him and his immediate family in order to seize power. After losing a wager with the penalty being wandering the forests for twelve years and an additional year incognito before returning to power, Arjuna and his family have returned to make their rightful claim on the throne. Their cousins refuse to hand over the throne, and so the time for open warfare has come.

He pauses at the edge of the battlefield, viewing the two sides of the family ready to fight. Feeling into the impending reality of fighting them, his conscience gives him trouble. He doesn't want to kill his kin, and he sees the assembled enemy army with compassion, recognizing the faces of loved ones and friends. He also fears that the motivation for this war, and therefore the ultimate flavor victory would have, is desire for power and possession of the throne. He tells his feelings to his charioteer and a dialogue ensues. His driver is none other than Krishna, who has not yet revealed himself as God, but has long been a trusted teacher and friend to Arjuna. Krishna instructs him to fulfill his duty as a member of the warrior class. While Arjuna understands his duty intellectually, he must come to terms with his conscience before he can fulfill it.

In the course of the dialogue, which takes place outside of time on the edge of the battlefield just prior to the beginning of the fighting, Krishna reveals himself in all his awesome, earth-shaking, mind-blowing splendor. Arjuna is duly impressed. He recognizes Krishna for the deity he says he is, and yet still requires guidance from Krishna and time with himself to work out the dilemma plaguing his conscience.

In the end, Arjuna accepts the teachings and instruction of Krishna (enumeration and analysis can be found in innumerable sources devoted to the *Bhagavad Gita*) and embraces his role in the events of the day. The dialogue ends and he steps into the battle in a frame of mind appropriate to one in his societal role as a warrior, embracing and embodying the teachings of his culture, family, and God.

What's All This About?

Essentially, the archetype of Arjunsuri is about taking responsibility for what one believes and how that belief manifests in one's life. When working with Arjunsuri, it is unimportant *what* people believe, only how they come to believe it and how their lives reflect it. There is in each of us a part that seeks the truest, most authentic outer expression of our internal reality, and each of us finds him- or herself at a different place in this process for a number of reasons, conditioning being the most prevalent.

Conditioning is how we were shaped by our families and cultures to become useful, compliant and productive members of those groups. We were taught ways of thinking, behaving and being that (for better or worse) in some ways grated against our individual natures. An Arjunsuri-inspired path or experience means breaking away from an established group and its directives, as this is a journey of individuation, of finding out what's true for one and how best to live a life that reflects that truth.

The story of Arjuna rests on his satisfaction that he is living the right kind of life, that he is behaving in a way that sits well with his conscience. When Krishna reveals himself in his awesome splendor, Arjuna doesn't immediately acquiesce. Make no mistake: Arjuna is terrified of the magnitude of this divine presence and in no way doubts that it's God in front of him, showing the lightning and shiny colors and the divine display of fireworks. However, just because God tells him to do something doesn't make that something right with his conscience. And if it's not right with his conscience, he can't do it.

Wait a minute – *God* tells him to do something and he doesn't do it? What could he possibly be thinking? Arjuna's living in a world in which personal responsibility is paramount. He knows that if he does something counter to his conscience, he'll create negative karma for himself. He doesn't jump when God says to, but he's willing to engage with Krishna in a dialogue about the whys and hows to make sure he understands what's being asked of him, and Krishna isn't in the least put off. How utterly reasonable they both are! This can sound absurd to Judeo-Christian ears, it shows us a critical lesson in personal responsibility those of us with such ears have probably not been taught.

So, where do we file this Arjunsuri business? In the "matters of conscience" file, not far from "self-discovery," "self-determination," and "self-direction." At root Arjunsuri is about coming to a right decision for ourselves about how we live our lives, regardless of what we have been told or are being told to do.

How Arjunsuri Differs from Jupiter and Uranus

We look at Jupiter in the natal chart to understand a native's belief system. While analysis of our Jupiter configurations does tell us about our capacity for belief and what sorts of things will appeal to us to believe in, Arjunsuri speaks to the process of how we arrive at what we believe. As a near-Earth asteroid with an orbit of 3.57 years, compared with Jupiter's orbit of roughly 12 years, its slant on questions of belief is more personal than that of Jupiter's.

During the stages of the process when there is little or no questioning and the outer life has not yet been brought to reflect the inner reality, Arjunsuri energy can appear to be a reinforcement of the native's Jupiter configuration – the business of belief proceeding as usual. It's when the experience of awakening is had, when the native learns the vital piece of information that changes everything in his or her mind, that what seems Jupiter-related emerges as something totally different and the energy of Arjunsuri becomes apparent.

We look at the Uranus configuration to understand one's capacity for and relationship to individuation, expression of freedom and how breaking out of established norms to create new levels of authentic living is done. Arjunsuri on the surface shares the individuation urge with Uranus, but Arjunsuri's act of breaking away is based in conscience. It is not an idea or an ideal, as we see with the mental energy associated with Uranus, but an action necessary to live in alignment with the highest truth of ourselves that we have access to at any given time.

Arjunsuri also isn't related to the problems inherent in structuring and organizing groups and the forfeiture of individuality that can follow, factors inspiring Uranian breaks with tradition and structure. The archetype is instead about breaking away *when necessary*, when it means living outwardly in more authentic ways to reflect an altered inner reality. Arjunsurian breaks can happen in a short time, even from one moment to the next, but carry none of the electricity of Uranian breaks. The former have the quality of a sudden knowing that things have already changed, while the latter present the need to break the chains of whatever association is undesirable or hindering expression. Said another way, Arjunsurian breaks are the physical manifestations of an inner reality that's already shifted, while physical Uranian breaks are often themselves changing reality and the information needed for the inner terrain to gain consciousness of what hasn't been working in the person's life.

The Archetypal Process – How We Live This Story

The Arjunsuri story as it plays out in our lives correlates to the mutable cross when viewed as an unfolding, four-staged process. We cycle through these stages repeatedly in each life and over the course of many lives. Within each life we might experience two or three of the stages again and again or cycle through all of them once or more than once, yet this can be separate from the overall soul journey. These are minor cycles within a greater cycle, with the conditioning of any one life setting the tone for the minor cycles of that life, and the overall trajectory of the soul's journey being that of the greater cycle.[1]

What we gain from the minor cycles of any life fills in gaps in our soul's understanding as we progress along the greater journey; no experience along this road is in vain. Very often, the real-world results from going back and forth from one stage to another repeatedly can inspire shame and embarrassment.

---

[1] Evolutionary astrology holds that the conditioning of the present life reflects a larger-scale conditioning of the soul; that any given life is reflective of karmic patterns. The cycles associated with Arjunsuri have details that differ in various lives, though the themes don't, and we can tend to make details of situations matter much more than their themes, even to the point of getting tripped up in a focus on the details. The Arjunsuri process offers opportunities to cease making details matter as what's deeply valued is the inner truth, which is always thematic in nature.

While it can be difficult for us to be forgiving and loving with ourselves when we make the same mistake repeatedly without understanding why, without feeling as though we have a useful perspective on our selves or actions, everything we learn about responsibility for belief along the way contributes to the overall journey.

The stages of the journey, whether we're talking minor or major cycles, follow the Mutable Cross when viewed as an unfolding process. Seen in this way, these four signs take us from questioning, observing and gathering data (Gemini) to analysis and critique (Virgo), then to employment of intuition and seeking the truth (Sagittarius), to acceptance, surrender and subsequent embodiment of the truth of the self as revealed by conscience (Pisces), after which the cycle is ready to begin again.

Gemini. Here we catalogue all possible bits of information without attempting to make sense of them. There's no structured worldview or guiding principle; this stage is that of exploration and curiosity, of amassing as many data as possible. From the Geminian perspective, nothing is truer than anything else because there is always another piece of data to be found around the next corner with the potential to change everything.

Virgo. This is the stage of classification, analysis and critique. This is the detail-oriented phase dedicated to sorting things out and deciding where they belong. The thinking in this stage is that a close enough look will reveal everything that's needed to be known, and truth is believed to be found in analyzing, tracking and comparing details.

Sagittarius. In the sign of the seeker, intuition comes into play. Candidates for what is true must pass a gut instinct, feeling test. The process of Sagittarius is the right-brained evaluation of possibly-true things and arriving at a stance of belief from a source of feeling about what is most likely true.

Pisces. The Pisces stage of the process is coming to surrender to the higher truth of what we are and therefore are comfortable serving. We accept that while we've spent perhaps a great deal of time and energy looking for, analyzing and evaluating possible contenders, the truth of what our conscience can comfortably be on board for has the entire time existed inside us. The Piscean phase is that of opening to and thereby embodying the truth of what we are that's been there all along.

Applied to the process of the Arjunsuri archetype, the Mutable Cross describes an arc of questioning styles. From within each stage, the motivation for questioning is very different, as are the expected and acceptable answers. Each phase of questioning will come from the bias of the stage one is in. When Virgo-style answers are offered in response to Piscean questions, a lack of connection occurs and the questioner is not possibly satisfied. Each of us has had the experience of seeking information and finding no source, whether human- or data-based, that provides answers that resonate with how and why we're asking them. It can look like a lack of chemistry or bad timing, and eventually will drive us either to throw our arms up in the air in resignation or desperation, or embark on a search for other, higher-level resources that may be able to answer our questions in more appropriate ways depending, as always, on our conditioning.

The main hang-up in each stage is a refusal to change, necessary to progress to the next stage. From the perspective of the larger soul cycle, there is no way to go wrong. Each stage has its self-defeating loop (Gemini can thrive on relativism, Virgo on nitpicking, Sagittarius on being right, and Pisces on being so open as to be unfocused and undirected), but the self-direction necessary to move through the stages is part of the work. Also, part of this work is existing in the places in between the stages, reflecting the process's fundamental relationship with the Mutable Cross.

Moving From Stage to Stage

In any given life, transitions from one stage to the next can be sudden and have the quality of epiphany. A person's perspective can change entirely in the blink of an eye, and the previous stage is, upon remarking that something has happened, left behind. Especially in the minor cycles, rarely is it a permanent arrival, as the part of us that's seeing our steps along this archetypal journey often must compete for center stage with the parts of us that are conditioned to avoid progress in such journeys. We're each full of sub-personalities, and they don't want to change.[2]

It is usually an external event that sheds new light on what's going on that triggers a change in phase. A person learns something about what is really happening in the environment or the truth of his her role in it, or the implications of either or both. Things come into a new, sharper focus. A bigger picture can be seen, and if there is any word from conscience to be had, this is where it will be heard. What if anything will be done after gaining the new knowledge is entirely up to the individual. In fact, it is at these times in our lives when, if we have not yet seen we have free will and are responsible for how our lives play out, we are shocked by the sudden awareness that we do. Equally shocking often is that we must make a choice in one direction or the other; we learn that the responsibility for the course of our lives is our own.

---

[2] Imagine being in the Virgo stage when it's time to move on to the Sagittarius stage: The control issues that can arise may be formidable.

In the major cycles, the movement is much slower. The soul learns over time the lessons of right questioning and authentic living in many different forms and guises, and as the majority of us do not retain conscious knowledge of prior-life experiences, we must to a degree relearn different sorts of lessons along the way. In time, with openness and commitment to the act of living a questioning and increasingly aware life, we will get in any given life back to the same point where left off in the greater soul journey and begin to make progress on it, that is to say begin working from within the same stage in the present life as we are in the multi-life process.

This feels like a groove we felt we were always looking for and we *finally* get to experience. A good rhythm that can be ushered in with new friends or teachers, new activities or stimulating pursuits that show us something critical about the world and our place in it. Our questions and how we think are understood and seen by others to matter, our interests are supported by those around us. This can be a thrilling time.

As the Arjunsuri story is ultimately about embodying an agenda and learning to take responsibility for how we live our lives, the work along the way is about doing, being and eventually showing – living out loud in some way. We may think we can avoid this work by not asking anything, not showing to or living around others what we believe, and even not admitting that we believe anything in the first place. This process can be put on hold for as long as we like, until eventually we actively step back into the process again, by choice or due to circumstances that look like anything but.

In periods of avoiding active participation in the journey, we're still operating according to the stage of the process we're in, and benefitting from what we experience. For instance, someone in the Gemini stage apparently opting out of the journey will still observe and be aware of what's going on around her, even if she makes no effort to retain what she's experiencing or seek out new knowledge. She's highly attuned to the work of Geminian phase and will see it around her for as long as she tries not to see it in herself. As with any archetypal energy we deal with in astrology, putting it out of our consciousness when it's time to deal with it will bring it back to us in the form of other people and external events; there's no avoiding what's on our life syllabus.

When we turn away from the truth our conscience reveals, we risk what amount to ruptures in our deepest connection to ourselves. Mental and physical illness can result from denying or steering away from these highly significant confrontations with personal truth. These can be mental and psychotic breaks, whether debilitating or not.

Physically, it can be a manifestation of illness that fits symbolically with the truth that the inner self is no longer able to be heard. The range of manifestations can be dramatic, including hearing and vision loss (making the statement that the higher self can no longer be heard or seen), ambulatory issues (the statement that the body can no longer head in any direction, given that the direction the higher self has shown is refused), and others.

When we accept the path conscience lays out for us, we announce a new level of maturity, on both the personality and soul levels. The result is a deeper connection to our innermost realities, an ability to create our outward lives according to parameters laid out by our innermost selves.

The Discovery Chart

Arjunsuri was discovered on March 24, 1998 by LINEAR at the Lincoln Lab facility of the Massachusetts Institute of Technology in Socorro, New Mexico. Its discovery is in my mind a wake-up call for us to open ourselves to the importance of personal responsibility about our beliefs and how we use them to create our lives and places in the world.

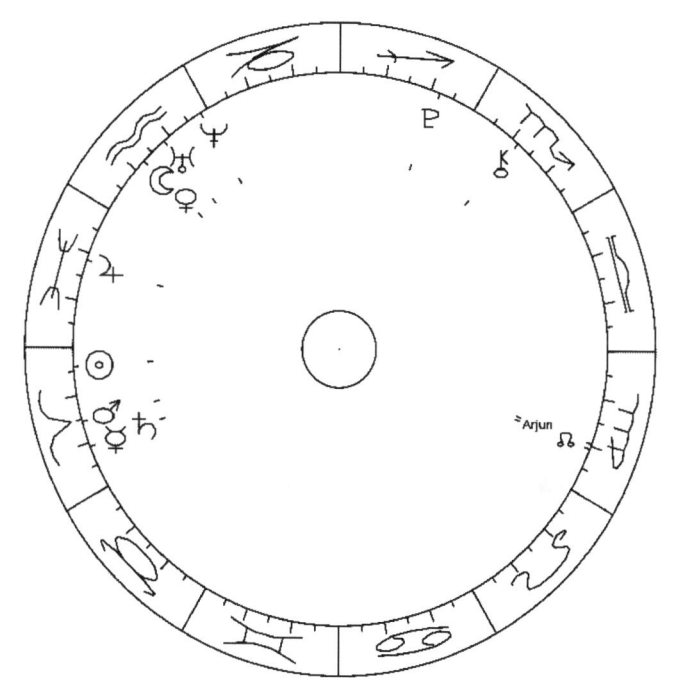

Arjunsuri Discovery Chart

Arjunsuri itself in the chart is retrograde and tightly conjunct the North Node in Virgo, opposing Jupiter in Pisces on the South Node. Square Arjunsuri and the nodal axis is retrograde Pluto in Sagittarius.

Arjunsuri relates to how we come to believe what we believe. In this chart the asteroid is opposite the traditional marker of belief, Jupiter, and in the sign of Virgo, indicating a need to begin being more critical and take more responsibility regarding our beliefs, a stance based more in discrimination and analytical thinking than in unquestioning acceptance. Its retrograde status echoes the call to personal, reflective truth seeking inside ourselves. Jupiter is in Pisces, indicating openness and acceptance surrounding beliefs, uncritical and perhaps blind. This planet in this sign on the South Node indicate that blind faith is the domain of the past, something we've done much of and cannot grow by pursuing – the South Node of the Moon represents our comfort zone. From the standpoint of evolutionary astrology, if we choose to stay in South Node symbolism we can be in many ways successful and feel safe, but never really happy or fulfilled, as evolutionary astrology views the mission of the soul as experience in the direction of growth, taking the best of what we know from our experience with the South Node symbolism and moving in the opposite direction with it. In this case, our willingness to believe is not something that should be left behind. The North Node is the area in which we are challenged to extend ourselves, to learn to stretch into, as it is foreign territory likely to be uncomfortable and frightening for us. In other words, our challenge is retain our capacity for belief and acceptance (Jupiter in Pisces on the South Node) while learning to question and think in critical ways (Virgo North Node) as we take responsibility for our beliefs and how we live them (Virgo Arjunsuri).

The emergence of this archetype into our consciousness seems a statement that it's no longer enough to live an excess of acceptance of received tradition. The beliefs we absorb from our environments (Jupiter in Pisces) no longer offer room to grow. In other words, our collective growth and evolution rests on learning to critically evaluate what we're told about what's true and take personal responsibility for how we live our lives.

Squares to the nodal axis in the evolutionary astrology paradigm indicate unresolved issues and will tend to be the focus of much attention. Some evolutionary astrologers see this focus as a distraction from overall growth, while others see it as a feature of the landscape, neither good nor bad but offering opportunities to learn. Some see that many people with squares to the nodes make them their occupations in life. The overall idea with these squares is that there's something about the energy we don't understand, and in our pre-occupation to figure it out, we will consequently draw to ourselves experiences and people who offer opportunities who might help us add the missing piece to our understanding.

With Arjunsuri on the North Node in Virgo opposing Jupiter in Pisces, the overall message is about a new level of responsibility and discrimination. Retrograde Pluto squaring the nodes from Sagittarius is a statement that we must dig deep inside ourselves to achieve that discrimination, to find out from deep inside what's really true. The square indicates that this deep digging will be a significant part of the journey. One way of thinking about this is that we need our recent, abundant examples of religious extremism and other Pluto-in-Sagittarius excesses to show us what we don't understand about the actual function and true place of belief in our lives.

Culturally speaking, we're gaining a view on several thousand years of our collective conditioning from monotheistic organized religions. I mean not to put these religions down, while I point out that there are loads of people who find out that such groups don't work for them, finding instead a call to go within to figure out what sort of approach will truly serve them. In fact, many find that organized religion of any kind doesn't work for them. The entrance of Arjunsuri into our cultural dialogue says that the way of the individual finding out what's true for him- or herself is the next stage in our evolution, but also that our collective evolution (NN) depends on individual evolution (the asteroid is retrograde on that NN). Depending on the circles you move in, you may have heard a lot about the recent arrival or coming of the Age of Aquarius, and the journey of the archetype of Arjunsuri naturally leads to a very Aquarian place.

Practical Applications

The key question when working with the Arjunsuri archetype in real-world, individual applications is "Is the agenda I'm serving serving me?" Below are several different categories of how this question plays out in people's lives, but you can apply this line of thinking to every arena of your life and the world around you.

Logos/Walking Ads
How comfortable are you being a walking advertisement for the manufacturer of your clothing and other things you buy? Have you noticed that shopping bags have gotten bigger and more colorful over the last few years?

Punching the Clock
A person may realize that the company they work for, or the industry they work in, is counter to what they want to support or pursue. Not everyone who experiences this will have an entirely negative experience. The realization that the work someone is doing is not going to take him where he wants to go can be liberating, and if the individual then moves into something more suited to his life direction, the resulting sense of fulfillment can be huge.

I used to work at a biotechnology company in an office related to the animal research groups. Very few lab personnel there hadn't seriously considered the reality of their work and its implications; there were no heartless, cruel people sticking animals with needles for kicks. A majority of them knew or were related to people with or who died from the diseases they were researching. Checking in with their consciences made them okay with what they were doing, and no matter how we might feel about their lab activities, they reflect healthy Arjunsuri work.

False Gurus

A great many people who have negative experiences with teachers and other sorts of leaders to whom they have become devoted will have prominent Arjunsuri configurations. We can allow the desire to believe to throw a shadow on the Arjunsuri process, leaving us aligning with someone that turns out to be an influence we need to get away from.

Religious Affiliations

This is a most recognizable arena of the Arjunsuri energy in our lives. The homosexual Catholic who refuses to be a member of a parish if it means denying or ignoring his or her sexuality, and the religious Jew of any nationality with problems of conscience based in Israeli politics are examples of Arjunsuri at work in people's lives. Examples abound in every faith where there can arise a discrepancy between the mandate of the group and the unique, personal realities of the individuals comprising the group.

Case Studies

Jiddu Krishnamurti

The most striking example of the Arjunsuri story I've found is that of Jiddu Krishnamurti, the renowned secular philosopher and teacher of the 20th century. As a young man, he was recognized and groomed by the Theosophical Society as the next World Teacher, a human to be trained in such a way as to prepare him to be vessel for the return of the Maitreya Buddha, akin in many ways in their minds to another Christ figure. He underwent extensive conditioning and training to adapt to this future role, including intensive studies in yoga, philosophy, and various occult disciplines. Krishnamurti for many years deferred to his teachers and what he was taught, never questioning and always affirming that he would do whatever was asked of him. While it's true that his devotion was due in large part to the nature of his bond with Anne Besant, president of the Society at the time (she was like a mother to him, and their devotion to each other was clear), it was his choice to be so pliable in service of the Society's cause.

Soon after his discovery and adoption by the Society, Besant formed a group called the Order of the Star to prepare the world for the unveiling of the World Teacher. Krishnamurti was made the president of the group, and his duties included traveling to chapters in various countries and speaking to the members.

Beginning in August of 1922, at the age of 27, he began having extremely intense pain that he later recognized as a cleansing by Ascended Masters integral to the process of preparing him for his future role. Numerous extended periods of such pain over the next seven years followed, and when he emerged from this, his willingness to be the instrument he'd been groomed to be was gone. None of the many years of conditioning appeared to have stuck. At its annual meeting of 1929 he disbanded the Order of the Star and in his now-famous statement told the three thousand members of the Order present that

> *Truth is a pathless land....A belief is purely an individual matter....Truth cannot be brought down, rather the individual must make the effort to ascend to it....You must climb towards the Truth, it cannot be stepped down or organized for you.*[3]

The statement he made that night set his agenda for the rest of his life. He taught from that day on that you can't learn the truth from a teacher, no one can do

---

[3] Krishnamurti: A Biography, Pupul Jayakar. Harper & Row: San Francisco, 1986, p. 75.

it for you. You must go down that path alone, and question and think for yourself.

Krishnamurti's natal Arjunsuri is retrograde in Scorpio in the 9th, conjunct retrograde Uranus in the same sign and house. It opposes his 3rd house Taurus Sun, squares the Aquarius-Leo horizon, and trines his 5th house Mars in Cancer.

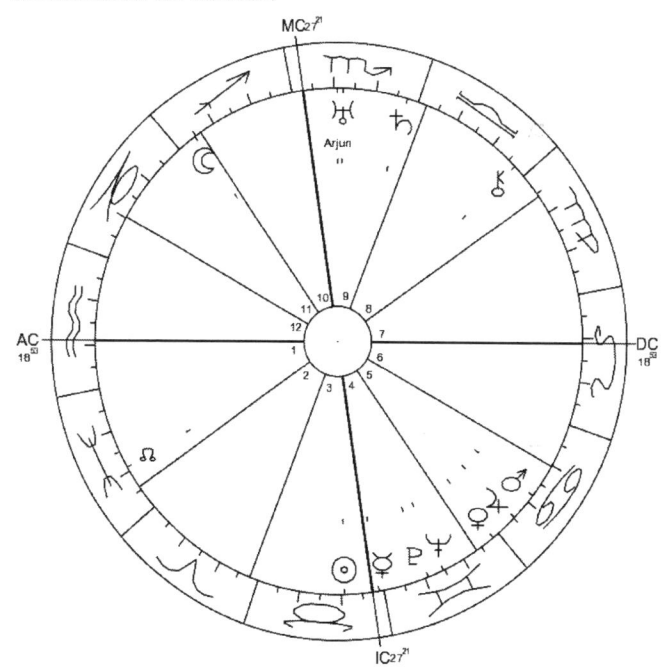

Krishnamurti's natal chart. May 12 1895, 12:30 AM, Madanapalle, India.[4] Rated AA.

---

[4] Krishnamurti: A Biography, p. 15.

With Arjunsuri opposing his Sun and squaring the horizon, I would expect him to be or appear malleable, but only up to a point, when the Arjunsurian shift makes a life change necessary. The horizon and the opposition in question occupy the fixed signs, which I believe has some part in why the conditioning never stuck. He operated in a compliant manner as his own needs to express his true nature (Sun in Taurus/3rd) were tangled up in not being sure about how to bring his own true nature out (opposing retrograde Arjunsuri-Uranus in the 9th and square the Ascendant-Descendant axis). Strange as it may seem to us, there was no reason to bring out his own philosophy or express his own ego nature until he was sure he no longer wanted to be associated with a spiritual group and further its aims, when he understood that such groups were fundamentally misconceived and entirely misguided. Not until this fixed grand cross was activated was there any reason to go against the teaching of the Society.

Precisely when his perspective changed between the onset of the pain in 1922 and the dissolution of the Order of the Star in 1929 is unclear. However, on the day he made the announcement, August 3, 1929, the transits paint a picture of stirring up his status quo.

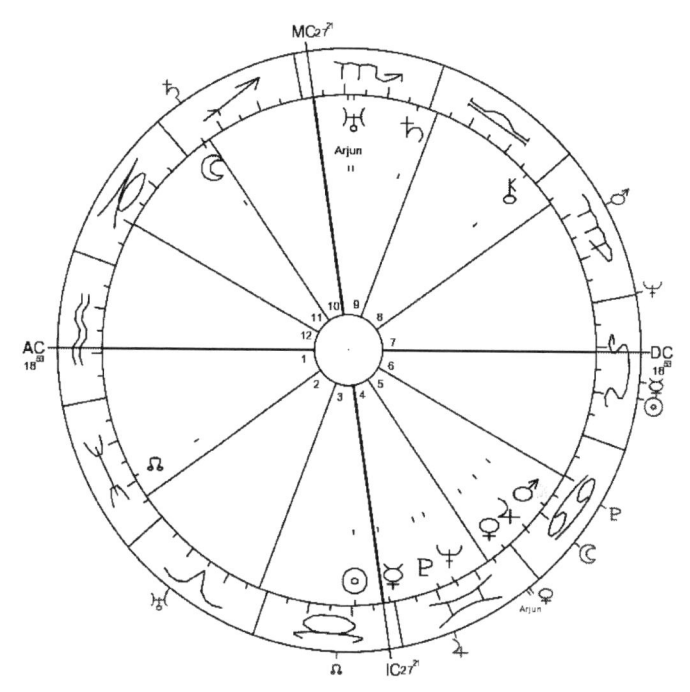

- Jupiter was conjunct his natal Pluto in the 4th, indicating an expansive influx of energy to his personal foundations.
- Mars sextiled his Arjunsuri and trined his Sun, energizing the opposition to natal Arjunsuri and Uranus with an urge to action.
- Arjunsuri itself was conjunct his 5th house Venus, calling for choice in personal expression rooted in conscience.
- Pluto trined his 9th house Arjunsuri-Uranus from the 5th house, supporting with expressive power the need to manifest outwardly what is known deeply within as truth.

- South Node was conjunct his 9th house Uranus, an influence sure to wake up that conjunction to make an original statement of his own beliefs.

Additionally, the conjunction of Arjunsuri-Uranus had by solar arc come to square his natal nodal axis, setting the stage to break out of the patterns of his habitual compliance in service to others (Virgo SN in the 7th). His progressed Moon was in Pisces in the 1st, conjunct his North Node, less than a degree applying. I see this as the trigger of the dissolution of the Order and the accompanying statement of philosophy that guided and was his foundation for the rest of his life. After so many years of being the symbol of other people's ideas, he vaulted into the symbolism of his North Node.[5] His fixed grand cross had been stirred to assert itself, and there was no turning back.

---

[5] The ruler of that North Node is Neptune in Gemini in the 4th, conjunct Pluto in Gemini. The path for him to come to a true acceptance of his true nature and stand up for it, assert the truth of his particular existence (NN in Pisces/1st), was made possible only after he inquired deeply into his own nature over the course of the years of his painful personal transformation (Gemini Pluto in the 4th).

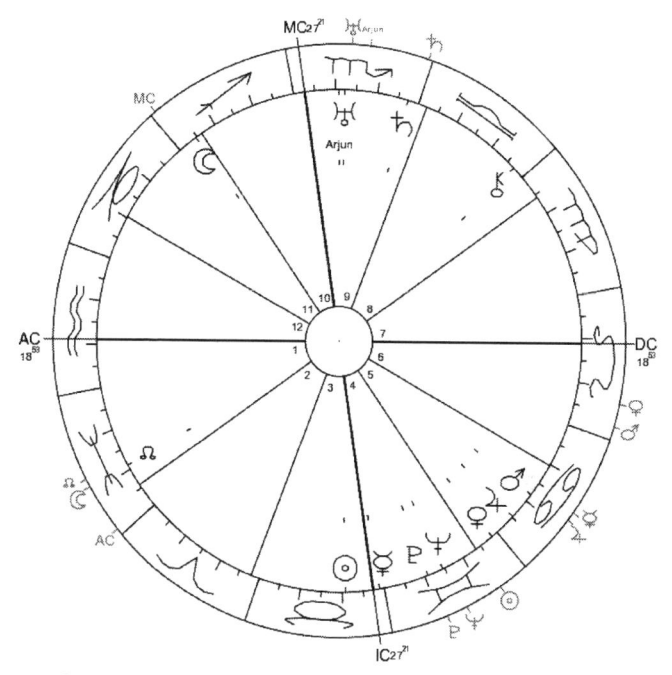

Krishnamurti progressions, August 3, 1929.

Not only does Jiddu Krishnamurti exemplify the awakening of the Arjunsuri archetype, the teaching he spent the rest of his life sharing fits with its message: The individual must seek truth within. He encouraged independent thought into the nature of a person's reality and the nature of belief, and told students and seekers to find their answers within themselves.

Additional Case Studies

A man with Arjunsuri conjunct his Sun-Neptune conjunction in Sagittarius in the 11th house [6] finds himself frequently, almost seasonally, questioning and evaluating whether his internal guidelines are getting him where he wants to go. When they don't, he initiates a restructuring of his entire philosophy of living, resulting in a shift in orientation to reflect more of what he's uncovered inside himself about who he is. His awareness of and familiarity with the Arjunsuri process startled me when I spoke with him about my research. The link with the Sun makes the mutable process of Arjunsuri central to his understanding of the idea of self.

Another man, with Arjunsuri conjunct Pluto and Venus in Virgo in the 11th house and Uranus in Leo in the 10th house [7] apprenticed himself to a meditation and spiritual teacher who formed a following that in time grew substantially, and who ultimately changed the nature of the group into what amounted to a cult. When the man awoke to the reality of the situation, he was a member of the teacher's inner circle (as one of his two bodyguards) and found himself faced with the decision to leave the community as it in no way

---

[6] November 30, 1973, 9:50 AM, San Francisco, CA, from birth certificate.

[7] July 16, 1962, 1:17 PM, Los Angeles, CA, from birth certificate.

reflected who he was. After thirteen years of dedication to the teacher and group, including many times dropping everything and moving across the country and changing professions at the direction of the teacher, his decision to leave was a major turning point in his life.

His awareness of the evolving nature of the group, and his unease and lessening trust in the teacher and the group's direction developed over several years. In March of 1993 he wrote a letter to the teacher detailing the reasons for his departure from the group. At the time, transiting Uranus and Neptune were applying to oppose his natal 9th house Cancer Sun, putting pressure on him to get clear on his sense of himself. His progressed Moon was directly opposing natal Arjunsuri, while his progressed Midheaven was conjunct his natal Uranus in Leo in the 10th, which is conjunct natal Arjunsuri with an orb of 3 degrees. His need to break away and create a life more aligned with his conscience had become unavoidable, as the call to create a place in the world more reflective of his actual needs was apparent.

Conclusion

As Pluto transited Sagittarius (1995-2008), we had many opportunities to get beneath the surface of what's going on and find our own reasons to seek our truth. Questions raised by this transit included, Where does fundamentalism get us, and how much of it can we take? What is the role of belief in our lives, and how do we use our beliefs to create our realities and our world? How is belief to be approached, navigated and manifested in our lives? And if we can get beyond the question of which belief is the right one, what responsibilities do we have to ourselves, each other and the greater community because of our beliefs? The discovery of the asteroid and the emergence of the Arjunsuri archetype into our collective consciousness offers the opportunity to build on what we've learned from Pluto's transit through the sign of the seeker. Pluto's ingress to Capricorn in early 2008 has offered opportunities to see how the structures we create in response to our Pluto-in-Sagittarius education may or may not work. Relative to Arjunsuri, the stage is set for people to find themselves underserved by their current, chosen Capricornian life structures and be open to Arjunsurian wake up calls to new levels of relating to their inner guidance systems.

An understanding of Arjunsuri and the archetypal process through the Mutable Cross can enable astrologers to understand how we come to believe what we believe. For anyone interested in finding and living according to a higher truth, Arjunsuri's energy and its mutable process of seeking will figure prominently in their lives and merits exploration.

About The Author

Tom Jacobs is an evolutionary astrologer, medium and channel with an active private practice with clients around the country and around the globe. A member of evolutionary astrologer Steven Forrest's Apprenticeship Program since 2004, his work supports people to uncover and connect deeply with what their souls are here to do.

His original work on the Lilith archetype and emotional healing are reflected in the two original natal reports available via his website, "The True Black Moon Lilith Natal Report" and "Living in the Present Tense: A Personalized Astrological 2012 Prep Course". He teaches karmic astrology and intuitive skills development both privately and to groups. Tom has a special interest in how health is affected by karma, including how we can improve our health by healing karma.

Tom holds a bachelor's degree in philosophy from The College of Wooster (Wooster, OH). He is the author of several books and his writings on astrology and spirituality have appeared in Dell Horoscope Magazine, Aspects Magazine, and InnerChange Magazine.

Contact Tom via his website, www.tdjacobs.com.

73119800R00083

Made in the USA
Lexington, KY
06 December 2017